DIARY OF AN OLD SOUL

DIARY OF AN OLD SOUL

GEORGE MACDONALD

INTRODUCTION BY LISA M. HESS

BARNES & NOBLE

NEW YORK

THE BARNES & NOBLE
LIBRARY OF ESSENTIAL READING

Introduction and Suggested Reading © 2006
by Barnes & Noble, Inc.

Originally published in 1880

This 2006 edition published by Barnes & Noble, Inc.

ISBN-13: 978-0-7607-8326-9
ISBN-10: 0-7607-8326-8

Printed and bound in the United States of America

1 3 5 7 9 10 8 6 4 2

Contents

INTRODUCTION

WHEN PREMATURE DEATH BECOMES TRAGIC LOSS, HOPE MAY YET BE found in the impassioned faith of a disciplined poet. Such contrasts come to life in the poetry of Scottish fantasy author, George MacDonald. His *Diary of an Old Soul* marks a yearlong poetic conversation with God in the face of the unexpected deaths of two of his children. Eavesdropping across the year, one can overhear MacDonald's spiritual longing within deep grief, the ebb and flow of a life within God's will, and grace amid the aridity of sorrow. He charts, in one stanza per day, the journey of a faithful heart confounded by tragic loss. He names the moments of felt presence alongside the apathy of felt abandonment. In poetic play and spiritual sincerity, he offers his own glimpses of creation, death, will, desire, and love. *Diary of an Old Soul* is one man's intimate spiritual journey through tragedy toward the multicolored hues of lived faith, where the Holy becomes beloved Friend and loving Father.

George MacDonald was born on December 10, 1824, as the second son of a Scottish Highlands farming family. Leaving his Highland roots for an education at King's College, Aberdeen, MacDonald brought his fervent love of nature and the Christian virtues into the intellectual worlds of literature and theology. He entered Highbury Theological College in 1848 to pursue his uncertain passion for Christian ministry. Meanwhile, he became engaged and married Louisa Powell, the daughter of a London merchant, upon acceptance of his first pastorate in the quiet little village of Arundel in the south of England. A serious bout of lung-hemorrhaging forced him to find retreat for recuperation on the Isle of Wight, where he wrote a 4,500-line poem, *Within and Without.* This offered him timely impetus to pursue a writing and teaching career when his rigidly Calvinist Arundel congregation found his theological views of God's compassion and ever-present grace heretical. The remainder of his life witnesses to a love of God, family, friends, and literature—the path of a joyous spirit, even in the face of persistent illness and intermittent poverty. Finding repeated safe harbor with friends, patrons, and publics who benefited greatly from his prosaic art and humbling orthodoxy, George MacDonald wrote over fifty volumes of fairy tales, fantasies, sermons, novels, and poetry. *Diary of an Old Soul* is his best-known volume of poetry, written in the late 1870s.

The narrative behind the *Diary's* publishing history compels attention today. Two of MacDonald's children, Mary Josephine and Maurice, died rather unexpectedly and within one year of each other. Newly engaged to be married, Mary suddenly took ill with a bronchial condition quite recognizable to the MacDonald family. George MacDonald himself was known for his frail health, particularly symptoms of tuberculosis, asthma, and eczema. He was recuperating from one of his own hemorrhaging bouts while he watched his twenty-five-year old daughter waste away. She died in 1878 within months of her initial symptoms. In similar fashion, with the weak bronchial health of the family and the difficult English air, Mary's younger brother, Maurice, took ill in 1879 and within three weeks died at age fifteen. Bearing his grief and ill health, MacDonald set himself the writing task of one seven-line poem per day, offered in wrestling conversation with a God he knew as loving Father yet who did not stay the hand of death for those so young. Originally titled *A Book of Strife in the Form of the Diary of an Old Soul*, this volume has been described as "one of the most remarkable records in all literature of an earnest soul's diligent and painstaking wrestling with the inexorable aspects of experience in order to discern God's presence and purpose."[1]

MacDonald eventually published all 366 stanzas (including one for February 29 in leap years) at his own expense. Unwin Brothers in London printed only a few copies, with limited distribution. The author John Ruskin received a copy as a gift from a mutual friend, Arthur Hughes, and praised it highly in his Oxford Lectures, thereby giving it some public awareness. An additional printing occurred in Chelsea in 1882, followed by a slightly larger printing by London's Longmans-Green in 1885. Various reprints assured the volume's survival until an American publisher, Augsburg Publishing House, picked it up under its contemporary title, *Diary of an Old Soul.*

With such a grief-born beginning and a small first printing with limited distribution, *A Book of Strife in the Form of the Diary of an Old Soul* initially reaped neither great public acclaim nor criticism. The popular view of the book slowly grew from Ruskin's literary acclaim until it became a recognized daily devotional resource. In comparison with the more scholarly, edited volume of MacDonald's poetry, *Diary of an Old Soul* offers an often painful, yet ultimately hopeful record of a parent's experience and wrestling in faith. MacDonald himself recognized the intimate character of this little volume with some trepidation. Hein writes, "MacDonald was well aware, but without the slightest trace of arrogance, that very few people are capable of entering into the intense spiritual longing after God and tender devotion to him that characterized his life."[2] Hein concludes that many readers find this compilation the most helpful and deeply comforting in the face of great loss and resulting grief.

MacDonald's poetic vision within *Diary of an Old Soul* does invite a renewed appreciation of the "jagged questions" of life. The entry for January 2, for example, gives MacDonald's patient awareness of light beyond the horizon and future understanding even amid painful questions. "A dim aurora rises in my east/Beyond the line of jagged questions hoar/ As if the head of our intombed High Priest/Began to glow behind the unopened door. . . ." His word choice is intimate, in the first person, as he feels the faithful hope of life beyond death. He names this hope in the risen Jesus, "our intombed High Priest" (according to the order of Melchizedek; Letter to the Hebrews 5:5–6), who died and yet comes to meet us from within the tomb on Easter morn. With such steeped, scriptural language and impassioned, natural imagery, this Victorian provokes our own awareness of love lived in death and home found only within the heart of God. The stanza yet concludes with a heaviness of heart: "Sure the gold wings will soon rise from the gray!/They rise not. Up I rise, press on the more,/To meet the slow coming of the Master's day." The light remains dim and we feel the burden of a sadness somehow content within the day governed only by God.

MacDonald unveils his own intimate awareness of the tender love of God, a primal love that invites a spiritual quest toward mystical union with God as loving Father, present Creator, lived Life. The entry for November 8 yields a seeker's yearning for such a love, alongside the pain of separation in Victorian notions of sovereignty. "My God, I look to thee for tenderness/Such as I could not seek from any man,/Or in a human heart fancy or plan—/A something deepest prayer will not express:/ . . . Until, . . . I yield the primal love, that no return desires." In other entries, MacDonald's natural imagery bespeaks this sovereign will, if in a merciful love. Water nourishes, yet in storm, it destroys. Fire inflames with life's desire, then painfully purifies the recalcitrant soul. Restless humanity wanders, sometimes flees, yet is ever welcomed homeward—a child to a mother's blossoming touch, an errant son befriended by God's obedient One. Ephemeral experiences of "winged faith," and prayers lofted into the heavens like birds into the air, scatter throughout MacDonald's poetic vision, urging all who will accompany him to pursue the restless quest anew. Undying love, made known in the graced mundane and trusted throughout the homelessness of doubt, beckons the reader to continue throughout a year's poetic discipline, offered in supple grief and "smooth resistless play."

George MacDonald spoke a vision of the eternal in the temporal by any means or genres available. His works include over fifty volumes of fairy tales, fantasy works, poetry, novels, sermons, and even some stage dramas. Hints of the English Romantics, such as William Wordsworth and Samuel Coleridge, and the Continental mystics, such as Emanuel Swedenborg and Jakob Böhme, can be found interwoven throughout these works. He had a special place in his heart for poetry, even though his father continually urged him to give up such foolishness, and began his poetry career in

1850. The poem previously mentioned, *Within and Without,* was received to high acclaim and he was labeled as a young poetic voice of some promise. It was also a saving grace during the next bout of hemorrhaging when poet Lord Byron's widow, Lady Byron, was so moved by the poem's spiritual force that she tracked down its author and afforded MacDonald a recuperative trip to Algiers.

His subsequent attempts at poetry were deemed inscrutable, so in 1858, MacDonald turned his attention to a "fantastic tale." The success of German fantasy writers (Frederick von Hardenberg or "Novalis" and E. T. A. Hoffman, in particular), the emergence of Charles Dickens' and William Thackeray's Christmas fantasies, and the acclaim for Hans Christian Andersen's fairy tales suggested to him that fantasy might be a suitable venture whereby he could support his family. By this time, MacDonald and his wife were living in Manchester, England, with three children and uncertain means to survive, especially considering his frail health. He found an immediate publisher for his new attempt, *Phantastes: A Faerie Romance for Men and Women,* and enjoyed the immediate financial support it provided. Yet the work was considered to be a colossal failure. The *Athenaeum,* a weekly literary review of the time, offered a scathing review, noting that every author is allowed one mistake and MacDonald had made his with this work. Discouraged, MacDonald looked to another genre of drama, this time to be fitted for the stage. Unable to find a publisher for his playwriting efforts, he responded with diligence to publishers' interest for novels.

MacDonald's skill as a novelist developed through many trials and failed beginnings over nearly a decade. His first published novel, *David Elginbrod,* was repeatedly refused until heavily supported by a popular novelist, Diana Maria Mulock, at her own publishing company, Hurst and Blackett. It was a huge success, garnering rave reviews from literary critics and resulting in over seven editions within MacDonald's lifetime, even more continuing up to this day. Thus began a successful career as a novelist, including his next attempt, *Adela Cathcart,* which folded into its plot children's fairy tales. A steady source of income emerged in 1859 with an offer to teach at Bedford College in London. MacDonald's interest and exploration in children's literature grew during this time, particularly as he developed a friendship with Lewis Carroll. Carroll finally published his now classic *Alice in Wonderland* only upon repeated urgings by the MacDonald family. From these educational and literary attempts, inspired by well-received Romantic and mystical authors, MacDonald wove together a body of work that was to fire the spirits and imaginations of adults and children alike.

MacDonald's occasional invitations to preach, his fairly rigorous lecture tours, and his increasing tenure within higher education also resulted in a couple volumes of published sermons and essays, particularly two famous essays noted as personally important to both J. R. R. Tolkien and C. S. Lewis: "The Imagination: Its Functions and Its Culture" (1867) and "The Fantastic Imagination" (1893). The *Unspoken Sermons* began in 1867 and while not as popularly received as his novels, or eventually as compelling as his fantasies and fairy tales, these sermons form the basis for a very popular compilation edited by C. S. Lewis, who claimed MacDonald as his spiritual mentor.

More and more a "literary theologian," MacDonald relied upon scripture yet had little interest in theological systems of belief. He found all of human experience to proffer possible grace and to serve as witness to the eternal, ever-present in the temporal. Truth was a person to MacDonald, not a creed or doctrinal proposition to be studied or debated. Human existence consisted of "being thought by God," the spiritual become incarnate in the beauty of God's creation and offered as sacrament to all seekers. In the face of a world fallen and tempted to evil, MacDonald yet spoke the story of the prodigal child enfolded in the arms of God, rediscovered as loving Father, Creator of all. Eventually, and much influenced by two similarly minded Anglican churchmen, F. D. Maurice and A. J. Scott, MacDonald did join the Church of England; yet his gentle orthodoxy assured him only marginal status as a religious thinker. His vision of the ideal human and of the quest to return home to the heart of the Creator God found expression instead in his storytelling. In fairy tale, fantasy, and theological novel, George MacDonald became a "theologian of literature" for generations of young and old to come.

MacDonald became an increasingly popular lecturer, even with his repeated bouts of hemmorhaging lungs, asthma attacks, and painful eczema. He toured England and the United States, where a friendship blossomed with Mark Twain and his wife, both of whom had read MacDonald's latest novel at the time, *Robert Falconer*, on their honeymoon. Health concerns in the entire MacDonald family—which now included eleven children—required regular and costly forays into more temperate climates, particularly Italy. Louisa MacDonald therefore invested her own creative endeavors to support the family as well, with a stage adaptation of the classic *Pilgrim's Progress*. The entire family drew together to perform this dramatic work for charge of admission, with George or his son Maurice playing the main character, Greatheart. They toured small churches and communities in both England and Italy, creating quite a stir at the time. After the death of Mary Josephine and Maurice, the whole family moved to Bordighera, Italy, where they became known for their lively intellectual and artistic hospitality. The MacDonalds continued to face financial pressures, but lived well into their seventies. Louisa died on January 13, 1902, in Bordighera. After moving to Ashtead in Surrey, England, George died September 18, 1905. His ashes are buried in Bordighera, alongside those of his wife.

George MacDonald arguably created the genre of fantasy before J. R. R. Tolkien distributed it worldwide (via the same original publisher of MacDonald's work here) and before C. S. Lewis offered non-allegorical commentary on it. Tolkien's *Lord of the Rings* trilogy, wildly successful in book reprints and in Peter Jackson's recent film homage, shows a clear inheritance of MacDonald's play with light and dark, shining and shadow, questing and home. One of MacDonald's last novels, *There and Back*, finds its echo in Tolkien's *The Hobbit: There and Back Again*. C. S. Lewis' *Narnia Chronicles*, gaining favor again in the recent film production, also suggest their fantastic roots in an imagination baptized by MacDonald's non-allegorical allegories of faith in *Phantastes* and *At the Back of the North Wind*. Images from MacDonald's work are found in such diverse literature as the poetry of T. S. Eliot and W. H. Auden, the children's stories of Maurice Sendak, and the narrative art of Madeleine L'Engle. The Inklings, the literary cohort that included not only Tolkien and Lewis but also Charles Williams, Dorothy Sayers, and others, lays claim to MacDonald as their literary "grandfather."

The recent one-hundred-year anniversary recognitions of MacDonald's work and the successes of his literary following have resulted in an increasing and deepening interest in this Victorian thinker, prophetic pastor, Scottish poet, and imaginative storyteller. His poetic passion, tended carefully within the rhythms of daily life, shows the spiritual journey to be a painful but life-giving grace: a continual opportunity to encounter the Holy in the mundane and a clear awareness of the real sufferings in loss. In *Diary of an Old Soul*, MacDonald proves to be a provocative and comforting companion for us all.

Lisa M. Hess teaches theology and ministry at United Theological Seminary in Dayton, Ohio. She is a Presbyterian minister (PCUSA), and she holds a Ph.D. in practical theology from Princeton Theological Seminary, where she was both lecturer and administrator for several years.

JANUARY

Oh, be thou then the first, the one thou art;
Be thou the calling, before all answering love,
And in me wake hope, fear, boundless desire.

January

One

LORD, WHAT I ONCE HAD DONE WITH YOUTHFUL MIGHT,
Had I been from the first true to the truth,
Grant me, now old, to do—with better sight,
And humbler heart, if not the brain of youth;
So wilt thou, in thy gentleness and ruth,
Lead back thy old soul, by the path of pain,
Round to his best—young eyes and heart and brain.

Two

A dim aurora rises in my east,
Beyond the line of jagged questions hoar,
As if the head of our intombed High Priest
Began to glow behind the unopened door:
Sure the gold wings will soon rise from the gray!
They rise not. Up I rise, press on the more,
To meet the slow coming of the Master's day.

Three

Sometimes I wake, and, lo, I have forgot,
And drifted out upon an ebbing sea!
My soul that was at rest now resteth not,
For I am with myself and not with thee;

Truth seems a blind moon in a glaring morn,
Where nothing is but sick-heart vanity:
Oh, thou who knowest, save thy child forlorn.

FOUR

Death, like high faith, leveling, lifteth all.
When I awake, my daughter and my son,
Grown sister and brother, in my arms shall fall,
Tenfold my girl and boy. Sure everyone
Of all the brood to the old wings will run.
Wholehearted is my worship of the man
From whom my earthly history began.

FIVE

Thy fishes breathe but where thy waters roll;
Thy birds fly but within thy airy sea;
My soul breathes only in thy infinite soul;
I breathe, I think, I love, I live but thee.
Oh, breathe, oh, sink—O Love, live into me;
Unworthy is my life till all divine,
Till thou see in me only what is thine.

SIX

Then shall I breathe in sweetest sharing, then
Think in harmonious consort with my kin;
Then shall I love well all my father's men,
Feel one with theirs the life my heart within.
O brothers, sisters holy, hearts divine,
Then I shall be all yours, and nothing mine—
To every human heart a mother-twin.

SEVEN

I see a child before an empty house,
Knocking and knocking at the closed door;
He wakes dull echoes—but nor man nor mouse,
If he stood knocking there forevermore.

A mother angel, see, folding each wing,
Soft-walking, crosses straight the empty floor,
And opens to the obstinate praying thing.

EIGHT

Were there but some deep, holy spell, whereby
Always I should remember thee—some mode
Of feeling the pure heat-throb momently
Of the spirit-fire still uttering this *I!*
Lord, see thou to it, take thou remembrance' load:
Only when I bethink me can I cry;
Remember thou, and prick me with love's goad.

NINE

If to myself—"God sometimes interferes"—
I said, my faith at once would be struck blind.
I see him all in all, the lifing mind,
Or nowhere in the vacant miles and years.
A love he is that watches and that hears,
Or but a mist fumed up from minds of men,
Whose fear and hope reach out beyond their ken.

TEN

When I no more can stir my soul to move,
And life is but the ashes of a fire;
When I can but remember that my heart
Once used to live and love, long and aspire—
Oh, be thou then the first, the one thou art;
Be thou the calling, before all answering love,
And in me wake hope, fear, boundless desire.

ELEVEN

I thought that I had lost thee; but, behold,
Thou comest to me from the horizon low,
Across the fields outspread of green and gold—
Fair carpet for thy feet to come and go.

Whence I know not, or how to me thou art come!
Not less my spirit with calm bliss doth glow,
Meeting thee only thus, in nature vague and dumb.

TWELVE

Doubt swells and surges, with swelling doubt behind!
My soul in storm is but a tattered sail,
Streaming its ribbons on the torrent gale;
In calm, 'tis but a limp and flapping thing:
Oh, swell it with thy breath; make it a wing,
To sweep through thee the ocean, with thee the wind
Nor rest until in thee its haven it shall find.

THIRTEEN

The idle flapping of the sail is doubt;
Faith swells it full to breast the breasting seas.
Hold, conscience, fast, and rule the ruling helm;
Hell's freezing north no tempest can send out,
But it shall toss thee homeward to thy leas;
Boisterous wave-crest never shall o'erwhelm
Thy sea-float bark as safe as field-borne rooted elm.

FOURTEEN

Sometimes, hard-trying, it seems I cannot pray—
For doubt, and pain, and anger, and all strife,
Yet some poor half-fledged prayer-bird from the nest
May fall, flit, fly, perch—crouch in the bowery breast
Of the large, nation-healing tree of life;
Moveless there sit through all the burning day,
And on my heart at night a fresh leaf cooling lay.

FIFTEEN

My harvest withers. Health, my means to live—
All things seem rushing straight into the dark.
But the dark still is God. I would not give
The smallest silver-piece to turn the rush

Backward or sideways. Am I not a spark
Of him who is the light? Fair hope doth flush
My cast. Divine success—Oh, hush and hark!

SIXTEEN

Thy will be done. I yield up everything.
"The life is more than meat"—then more than health;
"The body more than raiment"—then than wealth;
The hairs I made not, thou art numbering.
Thou art my life—I the brook, thou the spring.
Because thine eyes are open, I can see;
Because thou art thyself, 'tis therefore I am me.

SEVENTEEN

No sickness can come near to blast my health;
My life depends not upon any meat;
My bread comes not from any human tilth;
No wings will grow upon my changeless wealth;
Wrong cannot touch it, violence or deceit;
Thou art my life, my health, my bank, my barn—
And from all other gods thou plain dost warn.

EIGHTEEN

Care thou for mine whom I must leave behind;
Care that they know who 'tis for them takes care;
Thy present patience help them still to bear;
Lord, keep them clearing, growing, heart and mind;
In one thy oneness us together bind;
Last earthly prayer with which to thee I cling—
Grant that, save love, we owe not anything.

NINETEEN

'Tis well, for unembodied thought a live,
True house to build—of stubble, wood, nor hay;
So, like bees round the flower by which they thrive,
My thoughts are busy with the informing truth,

And as I build, I feed, and grow in youth—
Hoping to stand fresh, clean, and strong, and gay,
When up the east comes dawning his great day.

TWENTY

Thy will is truth—'tis therefore fate, the strong.
Would that my will did sweep full swing with thine!
Then harmony with every spheric song,
And conscious power, would give sureness divine.
Who thinks to thread thy great laws' onward throng,
Is as a fly that creeps his foolish way
Athwart an engine's wheels in smooth resistless play.

TWENTY-ONE

Thou in my heart hast planted, gardener divine,
A scion of the tree of life: it grows;
But not in every wind or weather it blows;
The leaves fall sometimes from the baby tree,
And the life-power seems melting into pine;
Yet still the sap keeps struggling to the shine,
And the unseen root clings cramplike unto thee.

TWENTY-TWO

Do thou, my God, my spirit's weather control;
And as I do not gloom though the day be dun,
Let me not gloom when earth-born vapors roll
Across the infinite zenith of my soul.
Should sudden brain-frost through the heart's summer run,
Cold, weary, joyless, waste of air and sun,
Thou art my south, my summer-wind, my all, my one.

TWENTY-THREE

O Life, why dost thou close me up in death?
O Health, why make me inhabit heaviness?
I ask, yet know: the sum of this distress,
Pang-haunted body, sore-dismayed mind,

Is but the egg that rounds the winged faith;
When that its path into the air shall find,
My heart will follow, high above cold, rain, and wind.

TWENTY-FOUR

I can no more than lift my weary eyes;
Therefore I lift my weary eyes—no more.
But my eyes pull my heart, and that, before
'Tis well awake, knocks where the conscience lies;
Conscience runs quick to the spirit's hidden door:
Straightway, from every sky-ward window, cries
Up to the Father's listening ears arise.

TWENTY-FIVE

Not in my fancy now I search to find thee;
Not in its loftiest forms would shape or bind thee;
I cry to one whom I can never know,
Filling me with an infinite overflow;
Not to a shape that dwells within my heart,
Clothed in perfections love and truth assigned thee,
But to the God thou knowest that thou art.

TWENTY-SIX

Not, Lord, because I have done well or ill;
Not that my mind looks up to thee clear-eyed;
Not that it struggles in fast cerements tied;
Not that I need thee daily sorer still;
Not that I, wretched, wander from thy will;
Not now for any cause to thee I cry,
But this, that thou art thou, and here am I.

TWENTY-SEVEN

Yestereve, Death came, and knocked at my thin door.
I from my window looked: the thing I saw,
The shape uncouth, I had not seen before.
I was disturbed—with fear, in sooth, not awe;

Whereof ashamed, I instantly did rouse
My will to seek thee—only to fear the more:
Alas! I could not find thee in the house.

TWENTY-EIGHT

I was like Peter when he began to sink.
To thee a new prayer therefore I have got—
That, when Death comes in earnest to my door,
Thou wouldst thyself go, when the latch doth clink,
And lead him to my room, up to my cot;
Then hold thy child's hand, hold and leave him not,
Till Death has done with him for evermore.

TWENTY-NINE

Till Death has done with him? Ah, leave me then!
And Death has done with me, oh, nevermore!
He comes—and goes—to leave me in thy arms,
Nearer thy heart, oh, nearer than before!
To lay thy child, naked, new-born again
Of mother earth, crept free through many harms,
Upon thy bosom—still to the very core.

THIRTY

Come to me, Lord: I will not speculate how,
Nor think at which door I would have thee appear,
Nor put off calling till my floors be swept,
But cry, "Come, Lord, come anyway, come now."
Doors, windows, I throw wide; my head I bow,
And sit like someone who so long has slept
That he knows nothing till his life draw near.

THIRTY-ONE

O Lord, I have been talking to the people;
Thought's wheels have round me whirled a fiery zone,
And the recoil of my words' airy ripple
My heart unheedful has puffed up and blown.

Therefore I cast myself before thee prone:
Lay cool hands on my burning brain, and press
From my weak heart the swelling emptiness.

FEBRUARY

Rest is but weakness, laughter crackling thorns;
If thou, the Truth, do not make them the true:
Thou art my life, O Christ, and nothing else will do.

FEBRUARY

ONE

I TO MYSELF HAVE NEITHER POWER NOR WORTH,
Patience nor love, nor anything right good;
My soul is a poor land, plenteous in dearth—
Here blades of grass, there a small herb for food—
A nothing that would be something if it could;
But if obedience, Lord, in me do grow,
I shall one day be better than I know.

TWO

The worst power of an evil mood is this—
It makes the bastard self seem in the right,
Self, self the end, the goal of human bliss.
But if the Christ-self in us be the might
Of saving God, why should I spend my force
With a dark thing to reason of the light—
Not push it rough aside, and hold obedient course?

THREE

Back still it comes to this: there was a man
Who said, "I am the truth, the life, the way"—
Shall I pass on, or shall I stop and hear?
"Come to the Father but by me none can":

What then is this? Am I not also one
Of those who live in fatherless dismay?
I stand, I look, I listen, I draw near.

FOUR

My Lord, I find that nothing else will do,
But follow where thou goest, sit at thy feet,
And where I have thee not, still run to meet.
Roses are scentless, hopeless are the morns,
Rest is but weakness, laughter crackling thorns,
If thou, the Truth, do not make them the true:
Thou art my life, O Christ, and nothing else will do.

FIVE

Thou art here—in heaven, I know, but not *from* here—
Although thy separate self do not appear;
If I could part the light from out the day,
There I should have thee! But thou art too near:
How find thee walking, when thou art the way?
O present Christ, make my eyes keen as stings,
To see thee at their heart, the glory even of things!

SIX

That thou art nowhere to be found, agree
Wise men, whose eyes are but for surfaces;
Men with eyes opened by the second birth,
To whom the seen, husk of the unseen is,
Descry thee soul of everything on earth.
Who know thy ends, thy means and motions see;
Eyes made for glory soon discover thee.

SEVEN

Thou near then, I draw nearer—to thy feet,
And sitting in thy shadow, look out on the shine;
Ready at thy first word to leave my seat—
Not thee: thou goest too. From every clod

Into thy footprint flows the indwelling wine;
And in my daily bread, keen-eyed I greet
Its being's heart, the very body of God.

EIGHT

Thou wilt interpret life to me, and men,
Art, nature, yea, my own soul's mysteries—
Bringing truth out, clear-joyous, to my ken,
Fair as the morn trampling the dull night. Then
The lone hillside shall hear exultant cries;
The joyous see me joy, the weeping weep;
The watching smile, as Death breathes on me his cold sleep.

NINE

I search my heart—I search, and find no faith.
Hidden he may be in its many folds—
I see him not revealed in all the world
Duty's firm shape thins to a misty wraith.
No good seems likely. To and fro I am hurled.
I have to stay. Only obedience holds—
I haste, I rise, I do the thing he saith.

TEN

Thou wouldst not have thy man crushed back to clay;
It must be, God, thou hast a strength to give
To him that fain would do what thou dost say;
Else how shall any soul repentant live,
Old griefs and new fears hurrying on dismay?
Let pain be what thou wilt, kind and degree,
Only in pain calm thou my heart with thee.

ELEVEN

I will not shift my ground like Moab's king,
But from this spot whereon I stand, I pray—
From this same barren rock to thee I say,
"Lord, in my commonness, in this very thing

That haunts my soul with folly—through the clay
Of this my pitcher, see the lamp's dim flake;
And hear the blow that would the pitcher break."

TWELVE

Be thou the well by which I lie and rest:
Be thou my tree of life, my garden ground;
Be thou my home, my fire, my chamber blest,
My book of wisdom, loved of all the best;
Oh, be my friend, each day still newer found,
As the eternal days and nights go round!
Nay, nay—thou art *my God,* in whom all loves are bound!

THIRTEEN

Two things at once, thou know'st I cannot think.
When busy with the work thou givest me,
I cannot consciously think then of thee.
Then why, when next thou lookest o'er the brink
Of my horizon, should my spirit shrink,
Reproached and fearful, nor to greet thee run?
Can I be two when I am only one?

FOURTEEN

My soul must unawares have sunk awry.
Some care, poor eagerness, ambition of work,
Some old offense that unforgiving did lurk,
Or some self-gratulation, soft and sly—
Something not thy sweet will, not the good part,
While the home-guard looked out, stirred up the old murk,
And so I gloomed away from thee, my Heart.

FIFTEEN

Therefore I make provision, ere I begin
To do the thing thou givest me to do,
Praying: Lord, wake me oftener, lest I sin.
Amidst my work, open thine eyes on me,

That I may wake and laugh, and know and see
Then with healed heart afresh catch up the clue,
And singing drop into my work anew.

SIXTEEN

If I should slow diverge, and listless stray
Into some thought, feeling, or dream unright,
O Watcher, my backsliding soul affray;
Let me not perish of the ghastly blight.
Be thou, O Life eternal, in me light;
Then merest approach of selfish or impure
Shall start me up alive, awake, secure.

SEVENTEEN

Lord, I have fallen again—a human clod!
Selfish I was, and heedless to offend;
Stood on my rights. Thy own child would not send
Away his shreds of nothing for the whole God!
Wretched, to thee who savest, low I bend:
Give me the power to let my rag-rights go
In the great wind that from thy gulf doth blow.

EIGHTEEN

Keep me from wrath, let it seem ever so right:
My wrath will never work thy righteousness.
Up, up the hill, to the whiter than snow-shine,
Help me to climb, and dwell in pardon's light.
I must be pure as thou, or ever less
Than thy design of me—therefore incline
My heart to take men's wrongs as thou tak'st mine.

NINETEEN

Lord, in thy Spirit's hurricane, I pray,
Strip my soul naked—dress it then thy way.
Change for me all my rags to cloth of gold.
Who would not poverty for riches yield?

A hovel sell to buy a treasure-field?
Who would a mess of porridge careful hold
Against the universe's birthright old?

TWENTY

Help me to yield my will, in labor even,
Nor toil on toil, greedy of doing, heap—
Fretting I cannot more than me is given;
That with the finest clay my wheel runs slow,
Nor lets the lovely thing the shapely grow;
That memory what thought gives it cannot keep,
And nightly rimes ere morn like cistus-petals go.

TWENTY-ONE

'Tis—shall thy will be done for me—or mine,
And I be made a thing not after thine—
My own, and dear in paltriest details?
Shall I be born of God, or of mere man?
Be made like Christ, or on some other plan?
I let all run—set thou and trim my sails;
Home then my course, let blow whatever gales.

TWENTY-TWO

With thee on board, each sailor is a king
Nor I mere captain of my vessel then,
But heir of earth and heaven, eternal child;
Daring all truth, nor fearing anything;
Mighty in love, the servant of all men;
Resenting nothing, taking rage and blare
Into the godlike silence of a loving care.

TWENTY-THREE

I cannot see, my God, a reason why
From morn to night I go not gladsome, free;
For, if thou art what my soul thinketh thee,
There is no burden but should lightly lie,

No duty but a joy at heart must be:
Love's perfect will can be nor sore nor small,
For God is light—in him no darkness is at all.

TWENTY-FOUR

'Tis something thus to think, and half to trust—
But, ah, my very heart, God-born, should lie
Spread to the fight, clean, clear of mire and rust,
And like a sponge drink the divine sunbeams.
What resolution then, strong, swift, and high!
What pure devotion, or to live or die!
And in my sleep, what true, what perfect dreams!

TWENTY-FIVE

There is a misty twilight of the soul
A sickly eclipse, low brooding o'er a man,
When the poor brain is as an empty bowl,
And the thought-spirit, weariful and wan,
Turning from that which yet it loves the best,
Sinks moveless, with life-poverty opprest—
Watch, then, O Lord, thy feebly glimmering coal.

TWENTY-SIX

I cannot think; in me is but a void;
I have felt much, and want to feel no more;
My soul is hungry for some poorer fare—
Some earthly nectar, gold not unalloyed—
The little child that's happy to the core,
Will leave his mother's lap, run down the stair,
Play with the servants—is his mother annoyed?

TWENTY-SEVEN

I would not have it so. Weary and worn,
Why not to thee run straight, and be at rest?
Motherward, with toy new, or garment torn,
The child that late forsook her changeless breast,

Runs to home's heart, the heaven that's heavenliest:
In joy or sorrow, feebleness or might,
Peace or commotion, be thou, Father, my delight.

TWENTY-EIGHT

The thing I would say, still comes forth with doubt
And difference—is it that thou shap'st my ends?
Or is it only the necessity
Of stubborn words, that shift sluggish about,
Warping my thought as it the sentence bends?
Have thou a part in it, O Lord, and I
Shall say a truth, if not the thing I try.

TWENTY-NINE

Gather my broken fragments to a whole
As these four quarters make a shining day.
Into thy basket, for my golden bowl,
Take up the things that I have cast away
In vice or indolence or unwise play.
Let mine be a merry, all-receiving heart,
But make it a whole, with light in every part.

MARCH

What if thou make us able to make like thee—
To light with moons, to clothe with greenery,
To hang gold sunsets o'er a rose and purple sea!

MARCH

ONE

THE SONG BIRDS THAT COME TO ME NIGHT AND MORN,
Fly oft away and vanish if I sleep,
Nor to my fowling-net will one return:
Is the thing ever ours we cannot keep?
But their souls go not out into the deep.
What matter if with changed song they come back
Old strength nor yet fresh beauty shall they lack.

TWO

Gloriously wasteful, O my Lord, art thou!
Sunset faints after sunset into the night,
Splendorously dying from thy window sill—
Forever. Sad our poverty doth bow
Before the riches of thy making might:
Sweep from thy space thy systems at thy will—
In thee the sun sets every sunset still.

THREE

And in the perfect time, O perfect God,
When we are in our home, our natal home,
When joy shall carry every sacred load,

And from its life and peace no heart shall roam,
What if thou make us able to make like thee—
To light with moons, to clothe with greenery,
To hang gold sunsets o'er a rose and purple sea!

FOUR

Then to his neighbor one may call out, "Come,
Brother, come hither—I would show you a thing";
And lo, a vision of his imagining,
Informed of thought which else had rested dumb,
Before the neighbor's truth-delighted eyes,
In the great ether of existence rise,
And two hearts each to each the closer cling!

FIVE

We make, but thou art the creating core.
Whatever thing I dream, invent, or feel,
Thou art the heart of it, the atmosphere.
Thou art inside all love man ever bore;
Yea, the love itself, whatever thing be dear.
Man calls his dog, he follows at his heel,
Because thou first art love, self-caused, essential, mere.

SIX

This day be with me, Lord, when I go forth,
Be nearer to me than I am able to ask.
In merriment, in converse, or in task,
Walking the street, listening to men of worth,
Or greeting such as only talk and bask,
Be thy thought still my waiting soul around,
And if he come, I shall be watching found.

SEVEN

What if, writing, I always seem to leave
Some better thing, or better way, behind,
Why should I therefore fret at all, or grieve!

The worse I drop, that I the better find;
The best is only in thy perfect mind.
Fallen threads I will not search for—I will weave.
Who makes the mill-wheel backward strike to grind!

EIGHT

Be with me, Lord. Keep me beyond all prayers:
For more than all my prayers my need of thee,
And thou beyond all need, all unknown cares;
What the heart's dear imagination dares,
Thou dost transcend in measureless majesty
All prayers in one—my God, be unto me
Thy own eternal self, absolutely.

NINE

Where should the unknown treasures of the truth
Lie, but there whence the truth comes out the most—
In the Son of man, folded in love and ruth?
Fair shore we see, fair ocean; but behind
Lie infinite reaches bathing many a coast—
The human thought of the eternal mind,
Pulsed by a living tide, blown by a living wind.

TEN

Thou, healthful Father, art the Ancient of Days,
And Jesus is the eternal youth of thee.
Our old age is the scorching of the bush
By life's indwelling, incorruptible blaze.
O Life, burn at this feeble shell of me,
Till I the sore singed garment off shall push,
Flap out my Psyche wings, and to thee rush.

ELEVEN

But shall I then rush to thee like a dart?
Or lie long hours aeonian yet betwixt
This hunger in me, and the Father's heart?

It shall be good, however, and not ill;
Of things and thoughts even now thou art my next;
Sole neighbor, and no space between, thou art—
And yet art drawing nearer, nearer still.

TWELVE

Therefore, my brothers, therefore, sisters dear,
However I, troubled or selfish, fail
In tenderness, or grace, or service clear,
I every moment draw to you more near;
God in us from our hearts veil after veil
Keeps lifting, till we see with his own sight,
And all together run in unity's delight.

THIRTEEN

I love thee, Lord, for very greed of love—
Not of the precious streams that towards me move,
But of the indwelling, outgoing, fountain store.
Than mine, oh, many an ignorant heart loves more!
Therefore the more, with Mary at thy feet,
I must sit worshiping—that, in my core,
Thy words may fan to a flame the low primeval heat.

FOURTEEN

Oh, my beloved, gone to heaven from me!
I would be rich in love to heap you with love;
I long to love you, sweet ones, perfectly—
Like God, who sees no spanning vault above,
No earth below, and feels no circling air—
Infinitely, no boundary anywhere.
I am a beast until I love as God doth love.

FIFTEEN

Ah, say not, 'tis but perfect self I want
But if it were, that self is fit to live
Whose perfectness is still itself to scant,

Which never longs to have, but still to give.
A self I must have, or not be at all:
Love, give me a self self-giving—or let me fall
To endless darkness back, and free me from life's thrall.

SIXTEEN

"Back," said I. Whither back? How to the dark?
From no dark came I, but the depths of light;
From the sun-heart I came, of love a spark:
What should I do but love with all my might?
To die of love severe and pure and stark,
Were scarcely loss; to lord a loveless height—
That were a living death, damnation's positive night.

SEVENTEEN

But love is life. To die of love is then
The only pass to higher life than this.
All love is death to loving, living men;
All deaths are leaps across clefts to the abyss.
Our life is the broken current, Lord, of thine,
Flashing from morn to morn with conscious shine—
Then first by willing death self-made, then life divine.

EIGHTEEN

I love you, my sweet children, who are gone
Into another mansion; but I know
I love you not as I shall love you yet.
I love you, sweet dead children; there are none
In the land to which ye vanished to go,
Whose hearts more truly on your hearts are set—
Yet should I die of grief to love you only so.

NINETEEN

"I am but a beast before thee, Lord."
Great poet-king, I thank thee for the word.
Leave not thy son half-made in beastly guise—

Less than a man, with more than human cries—
An unshaped thing in which thyself cries out!
Finish me, Father; now I am but a doubt;
Oh, make thy moaning thing for joy to reap and shout!

TWENTY

Let my soul talk to thee in ordered words,
O King of kings, O Lord of only lords!
When I am thinking thee within my heart,
From the broken reflex be not far apart.
The troubled water, dim with upstirred soil,
Makes not the image which it yet can spoil:
Come nearer, Lord, and smooth the wrinkled coil.

TWENTY-ONE

O Lord, when I do think of my departed,
I think of thee who art the death of parting;
Of him who crying Father breathed his last,
Then radiant from the sepulchre upstarted.
Even then, I think, thy hands and feet kept smarting:
With us the bitterness of death is past,
But by the feet he still doth hold us fast.

TWENTY-TWO

Therefore our hands thy feet do hold as fast.
We pray not to be spared the sorest pang,
But only—be thou with us to the last.
Let not our heart be troubled at the clang
Of hammer and nails, nor dread the spear's keen fang,
Nor the ghast sickening that comes of pain,
Nor yet the last clutch of the banished brain.

TWENTY-THREE

Lord, pity us: we have no making power;
Then give us making will, adopting thine.
Make, make, and make us; temper, and refine.

Be in us patience—neither to start nor cower.
Christ, if thou be not with us—not by sign,
But presence, actual as the wounds that bleed—
We shall not bear it, but shall die indeed.

TWENTY-FOUR

O Christ, have pity on all men when they come
Unto the border haunted of dismay;
When that they know not draweth very near—
The other thing, the opposite of day,
Formless and ghastly, sick, and gaping-dumb,
Before which even love doth lose his cheer:
O radiant Christ, remember then thy fear.

TWENTY-FIVE

Be by me, Lord, this day. Thou know'st I mean—
Lord, make me mind thee. I herewith forestall
My own forgetfulness, when I stoop to glean
The corn of earth—which yet *thy* hand lets fall.
Be for me then against myself. Oh, lean
Over me then when I invert my cup;
Take me, if by the hair, and lift me up.

TWENTY-SIX

Lord of essential life, help me to die.
To will to die is one with highest life,
The mightiest act that to will's hand doth lie—
Born of God's essence, and of man's hard strife:
God, give me strength my evil self to kill,
And die into the heaven of thy pure will.
Then shall this body's death be very tolerable.

TWENTY-SEVEN

As to our mothers came help in our birth—
Not lost in lifing us, but saved and blest—
Self bearing self, although right sorely prest,

Shall nothing lose, but die and be at rest
In life eternal, beyond all care and dearth.
God-born then truly, a man does no more ill,
Perfectly loves, and has whate'er he will.

TWENTY-EIGHT

As our dear animals do suffer less
Because their pain spreads neither right nor left,
Lost in oblivion and foresightlessness—
Our suffering sore by faith shall be bereft
Of all dismay, and every weak excess.
His presence shall be better in our pain,
Than even self-absence to the weaker brain.

TWENTY-NINE

"Father, let this cup pass." He prayed—was heard.
What cup was it that passed away from him?
Sure not the death-cup, now filled to the brim!
There was no quailing in the awful word;
He still was King of kings, of lords the Lord—
He feared lest, in the suffering waste and grim,
His faith might grow too faint and sickly dim.

THIRTY

Thy mind, my Master, I will dare explore;
What we are told, that we are meant to know.
Into thy soul I search yet more and more,
Led by the lamp of my desire and woe.
If thee, my Lord, I may not understand,
I am a wanderer in a houseless land,
A weeping thirst by hot winds ever fanned.

THIRTY-ONE

Therefore I look again—and think I see
That, when at last he did cry out, "My God,
Why hast thou me forsaken?" straight man's rod

Was turned aside; for, that same moment, he
Cried "Father!" and gave up will and breath and spirit
Into his hands whose all he did inherit—
Delivered, glorified eternally.

APRIL

Thou lovest perfectly—that is thy bliss:
We must love like thee, or our being miss—
So, to love perfectly, love perfect Love, love thee.

APRIL

ONE

LORD, I DO CHOOSE THE HIGHER THAN MY WILL.
I would be handled by thy nursing arms
After thy will, not my infant alarms.
Hurt me thou wilt—but then more loving still,
If more can be and less, in love's perfect zone!
My fancy shrinks from least of all thy harms,
But do thy will with me—I am thine own.

TWO

Some things wilt thou not one day turn to dreams?
Some dreams wilt thou not one day turn to fact?
The thing that painful, more than should be, seems,
Shall not thy sliding years with them retract—
Shall fair realities not counteract?
The thing that was well dreamed of bliss and joy—
Wilt thou not breathe thy life into the toy?

THREE

I have had dreams of absolute delight,
Beyond all waking bliss—only of grass,
Flowers, wind, a peak, a limb of marble white;
They dwell with me like things half come to pass,

True prophecies—when I with thee am right,
If I pray, waking, for such a joy of sight,
Thou with the gold, wilt not refuse the brass.

FOUR

I think I shall not ever pray for such;
Thy bliss will overflood my heart and brain,
And I want no unripe things back again.
Love ever fresher, lovelier than of old—
How should it want its more exchanged for much?
Love will not backward sigh, but forward strain,
On in the tale still telling, never told.

FIVE

What has been, shall not only be, but is.
The hues of dreamland, strange and sweet and tender
Are but hint-shadows of full many a splendor
Which the high Parent-love will yet unroll
Before his child's obedient, humble soul.
Ah me, my God, in thee lies every bliss
Whose shadow men go hunting wearily amiss.

SIX

Now, ere I sleep, I wonder what I shall dream.
Some sense of being, utter new, may come
Into my soul while I am blind and dumb—
With shapes and airs and scents which dark hours teem,
Of other sort than those that haunt the day,
Hinting at precious things, ages away
In the long tale of us God to himself doth say.

SEVEN

Late, in a dream, an unknown lady I saw
Stand on a tomb; down she to me stepped thence.
"They tell me," quoth I, "thou art one of the dead!"
And scarce believed for gladness the yea she said;

A strange auroral bliss, an arctic awe,
A new, outworldish joy awoke intense,
To think I talked with one that verily was dead.

EIGHT

Thou dost demand our love, holy Lord Christ,
And batest nothing of thy modesty;
Thou know'st no other way to bliss the highest
Than loving thee, the loving, perfectly.
Thou lovest perfectly—that is thy bliss:
We must love like thee, or our being miss—
So, to love perfectly, love perfect Love, love thee.

NINE

Here is my heart, O Christ; thou know'st I love thee.
But wretched is the thing I call my love.
O Love divine, rise up in me and move me—
I follow surely when thou first dost move.
To love the perfect love, is primal, mere
Necessity; and he who holds life dear,
Must love thee every hope and heart above.

TEN

Might I but scatter interfering things—
Questions and doubts, distrusts and anxious pride,
And in thy garment, as under gathering wings,
Nestle obedient to thy loving side,
Easy it were to love thee. But when thou
Send'st me to think and labor from thee wide,
Love falls to asking many a why and how.

ELEVEN

Easier it were, but poorer were the love.
Lord, I would have me love thee from the deeps—
Of troubled thought, of pain, of weariness.
Through seething wastes below, billows above,

My soul should rise in eager, hungering leaps;
Through thorny thicks, through sands unstable press—
Out of my dream to him who slumbers not nor sleeps.

TWELVE

I do not fear the greatness of thy command—
To keep heart-open-house to brother men;
But till in thy God's love perfect I stand,
My door not wide enough will open. Then
Each man will be love-awful in my sight;
And, open to the eternal morning's might,
Each human face will shine my window for thy light.

THIRTEEN

Make me all patience and all diligence;
Patience, that thou mayst have thy time with me;
Diligence, that I waste not thy expense
In sending out to bring me home to thee.
What though thy work in me transcends my sense—
Too fine, too high, for me to understand—
I hope entirely. On, Lord, with thy labor grand.

FOURTEEN

Lest I be humbled at the last, and told
That my great labor was but for my peace
That not for love or truth had I been bold,
But merely for a prisoned heart's release;
Careful, I humble me now before thy feet:
Whate'er I be, I cry, and will not cease—
Let me not perish, though favor be not meet.

FIFTEEN

For, what I seek thou knowest I must find,
Or miserably die for lack of love.
I justify thee: what is in thy mind,
If it be shame to me, all shame above.

Thou know'st I choose it—know'st I would not shove
The hand away that stripped me for the rod—
If so it pleased my Life, my love-made-angry God.

SIXTEEN

I see a door, a multitude near by,
In creed and quarrel, sure disciples all!
Gladly they would, they say, enter the hall,
But cannot, the stone threshold is so high.
From unseen hand, full many a feeding crumb,
Slow dropping o'er the threshold high doth come:
They gather and eat, with much disputing hum.

SEVENTEEN

Still and anon, a loud clear voice doth call—
"Make your feet clean, and enter so the hall."
They hear, they stoop, they gather each a crumb.
Oh, the deaf people! Would they were also dumb!
Hear how they talk, and lack of Christ deplore,
Stamping with muddy feet about the door,
And will not wipe them clean to walk upon his floor!

EIGHTEEN

But see, one comes; he listens to the voice;
Careful he wipes his weary dusty feet!
The voice hath spoken—to him is left no choice;
He hurries to obey—that only is meet.
Low sinks the threshold, leveled with the ground;
The man leaps in—to liberty he's bound.
The rest go talking, walking, picking round.

NINETEEN

If I, thus writing, rebuke my neighbor dull,
And talk, and write, and enter not the door,
Than all the rest I wrong Christ tenfold more,
Making his gift of vision void and null.

Help me this day to be thy humble sheep,
Eating thy grass, and following, thou before;
From wolfish lies my life, O Shepherd, keep.

TWENTY

God, help me, dull of heart, to trust in thee.
Thou art the Father of me—not any mood
Can part me from the *One*, the verily *Good*.
When fog and failure o'er my being brood,
When life looks but a glimmering marshy clod,
No fire out flashing from the living God—
Then, then, to rest in faith were worthy victory!

TWENTY-ONE

To trust is gain and growth, not mere sown seed!
Faith heaves the world round to the heavenly dawn,
In whose great light the soul doth spell and read
Itself high-born, its being derived and drawn
From the eternal self-existent fire;
Then, mazed with joy of its own heavenly breed,
Exultant-humble falls before its awful sire.

TWENTY-TWO

Art thou not, Jesus, busy like to us?
Thee shall I image as one sitting still,
Ordering all things in thy potent will,
Silent, and thinking ever to thy Father,
Whose thought through thee flows multitudinous?
Or shall I think of thee as journeying, rather,
Ceaseless through space, because thou everything dost fill?

TWENTY-THREE

That all things thou dost fill, I well may think—
Thy power doth reach me in so many ways.
Thou who in one the universe dost bind,
Passest through all the channels of my mind;

The sun of thought, across the farthest brink
Of consciousness thou sendest me thy rays;
Nor drawest them in when lost in sleep I sink.

TWENTY-FOUR

So common are thy paths, thy coming seems
Only another phase oft of my *me;*
But nearer is my *I,* O Lord, to thee,
Than is my *I* to what itself it deems;
How better then couldst thou, O Master, come,
Than from thy home across into my home,
Straight o'er the marches that I cannot see!

TWENTY-FIVE

Marches? 'Twixt thee and me there's no division,
Except the meeting of thy will and mine,
The loves that love, the wills that will the same.
Where thine meets mine is my life's true condition;
Yea, only there it burns with any flame.
Thy will but holds me to my life's fruition.
O God, I would—I have no mine that is not thine.

TWENTY-SIX

I look for thee, and do not see thee come.
If I could see thee, 'twere a commoner thing,
And shallower comfort would thy coming bring.
Earth, sea, and air lie round me moveless dumb,
Never a tremble, an expectant hum,
To tell the Lord of hearts is drawing near:
Lo, in the looking eyes, the looked for Lord is here.

TWENTY-SEVEN

I take a comfort from my very badness:
It is for lack of thee that I am bad.
How close, how infinitely closer yet
Must I come to thee, ere I can pay one debt

Which mere humanity has on me set!
"How close to thee!" No wonder, soul, thou art glad!
Oneness with him is the eternal gladness.

TWENTY-EIGHT

What can there be so close as *making* and *made?*
Nought twinned can be so near; thou art more nigh
To me, my God, than is this thinking *I*
To that I mean when *I* by me is said;
Thou art more near me, than is my ready will
Near to my love, though both one place do fill;
Yet, till we are one, ah me, the long *until!*

TWENTY-NINE

Then shall my heart behold thee everywhere.
The vision rises of a speechless thing,
A perfectness of bliss beyond compare!
A time when I nor breathe nor think nor move,
But I do breathe and think and feel thy love,
The soul of all the songs the saints do sing!
And life dies out in bliss, to come again in prayer.

THIRTY

In the great glow of that great love, this death
Would melt away like a fantastic cloud;
I should no more shrink from it than from the breath
That makes in the frosty air a nimbus-shroud;
Thou, Love, hast conquered death, and I aloud
Should triumph over him, with thy saintly crowd,
That where the Lamb goes ever followeth.

MAY

How rulest thou from the undiscovered bourn
The world-wise world that laughs thee still to scorn?
Please, Lord, let thy disciple understand.

MAY

ONE

WHAT THOUGH MY WORDS GLANCE SIDEWAYS FROM THE THING
Which I would utter in thine ear, my sire!
Truth in the inward parts thou dost desire—
Wise hunger, not a fitness fine of speech:
The little child that clamoring fails to reach
With upstretched hand the fringe of her attire,
Yet meets the mother's hand down hurrying.

TWO

Even when their foolish words they turned on him,
He did not his disciples send away;
He knew their hearts were foolish, eyes were dim,
And therefore by his side needs must they stay.
Thou wilt not, Lord, send me away from thee.
When I am foolish, make thy cock crow grim;
If that is not enough, turn, Lord, and look on me.

THREE

Another day of gloom and slanting rain!
Of closed skies, cold winds, and blight and bane!
Such not the weather, Lord, which thou art fain
To give thy chosen, sweet to heart and brain!

Until we mourn, thou keep'st the merry tune;
Thy hand unloved its pleasure must restrain,
Nor spoil both gift and child by lavishing too soon.

FOUR

But all things shall be ours! Up, heart, and sing.
All things were made for us—we are God's heirs—
Moon, sun, and wildest comets that do trail
A crowd of small worlds for a swiftness-tail!
Up from thy depths in me, my child-heart bring—
The child alone inherits anything:
God's little children-gods—all things are theirs!

FIVE

Thy great deliverance is a greater thing
Than purest imagination can foregrasp;
A thing beyond all conscious hungering,
Beyond all hope that makes the poet sing.
It takes the clinging world, undoes its clasp,
Floats it afar upon a mighty sea,
And leaves us quiet with love and liberty and thee.

SIX

Through all the fog, through all earth's wintry sighs,
I scent thy spring, I feel the eternal air,
Warm, soft, and dewy, filled with flowery eyes,
And gentle, murmuring motions everywhere—
Of life in heart, and tree, and brook, and moss;
Thy breath wakes beauty, love, and bliss, and prayer,
And strength to hang with nails upon thy cross.

SEVEN

If thou hadst closed my life in seed and husk,
And cast me into soft, warm, damp, dark mold,
All unaware of light come through the dusk,
I yet should feel the split of each shelly fold,

Should feel the growing of my prisoned heart,
And dully dream of being slow unrolled,
And in some other vagueness taking part.

EIGHT

And little as the world I should foreknow
Up into which I was about to rise—
Its rains, its radiance, airs, and warmth, and skies,
How it would greet me, how its wind would blow—
As little, it may be, I do know the good
Which I for years half darkling have pursued—
The second birth for which my nature cries.

NINE

The life that knows not, patient waits, nor longs—
I know, and would be patient, yet would long.
I can be patient for all coming songs,
But let me sing my one monotonous song.
To me the time is slow my mold among;
To quicker life I fain would spur and start
The aching growth at my dull-swelling heart.

TEN

Christ is the pledge that I shall one day see;
That one day, still with him, I shall awake,
And know my God, at one with him and free.
O lordly essence, come to life in me;
The will-throb let me feel that doth me make;
Now have I many a mighty hope in thee,
Then shall I rest although the universe should quake.

ELEVEN

Haste to me, Lord, when this fool-heart of mine
Begins to gnaw itself with selfish craving;
Or, like a foul thing scarcely worth the saving,
Swoln up with wrath, desireth vengeance fine.

Haste, Lord, to help, when reason favors wrong;
Haste when thy soul, the high-born thing divine,
Is torn by passion's raving, maniac throng.

TWELVE

Fair freshness of the God-breathed spirit air,
Pass through my soul, and make it strong to love;
Wither with gracious cold what demons dare
Shoot from my hell into my world above;
Let them drop down, like leaves the sun doth sear,
And flutter far into the inane and bare,
Leaving my middle-earth calm, wise, and clear.

THIRTEEN

Even thou canst give me neither thought nor thing,
Were it the priceless pearl hid in the land,
Which, if I fix thereon a greedy gaze,
Becomes not poison that doth burn and cling;
Their own bad look my foolish eyes doth daze,
They see the gift, see not the giving hand—
From the living root the apple dead I wring.

FOURTEEN

This versing, even the reading of the tale
That brings my heart its joy unspeakable,
Sometimes will softly, unsuspectedly hale
That heart from thee, and all its pulses quell.
Discovery's pride, joy's bliss, take aback my sail,
And sweep me from thy presence and my grace,
Because my eyes dropped from the Master's face.

FIFTEEN

Afresh I seek thee. Lead me—once more I pray—
Even should it be against my will, thy way.
Let me not feel thee foreign any hour,
Or shrink from thee as an estranged power.

Through doubt, through faith, through bliss, through stark dismay,
Through sunshine, wind, or snow, or fog, or shower,
Draw me to thee who art my only day.

SIXTEEN

I would go near thee—but I cannot press
Into thy presence—it helps not to presume.
Thy doors are deeds; the handles are their doing.
He whose day-life is obedient righteousness,
Who, after failure, or a poor success,
Rises up, stronger effort yet renewing
He finds thee, Lord, at length, in his own common room.

SEVENTEEN

Lord, thou hast carried me through this evening's duty;
I am released, weary, and well content.
O soul, put on the evening dress of beauty,
Thy sunset-flush, of gold and purple blent!
Alas, the moment I turn to my heart,
Feeling runs out of doors, or stands apart,
But such as I am, Lord, take me as thou art.

EIGHTEEN

The word he then did speak, fits now as then,
For the same kind of men doth mock at it.
God-fools, God-drunkards these do call the men
Who think the poverty of their all not fit,
Borne humbly by their art, their voice, their pen,
Save for its allness, at thy feet to fling,
For whom all is unfit that is not everything.

NINETEEN

O Christ, my life, possess me utterly.
Take me and make a little Christ of me.
If I am anything but thy Father's son,
'Tis something not yet from the darkness won.

Oh, give me light to live with open eyes.
Oh, give me life to hope above all skies.
Give me thy spirit to haunt the Father with my cries.

TWENTY

'Tis hard for man to rouse his spirit up—
It is the human creative agony,
Though but to hold the heart an empty cup,
Or tighten on the team the rigid rein.
Many will rather lie among the slain
Than creep through narrow ways the light to gain—
Than wake the will, and be born bitterly.

TWENTY-ONE

But he who would be born again indeed,
Must wake his soul unnumbered times a day,
And urge himself to life with holy greed;
Now ope his bosom to the wind's free play;
And now, with patience forceful, hard, lie still,
Submiss and ready to the making will,
Athirst and empty, for God's breath to fill.

TWENTY-TWO

All times are thine whose will is our remede.
Man turns to thee, thou hast not turned away;
The look he casts, thy labor that did breed—
It is thy work, thy business all the day:
That look, not foregone fitness, thou dost heed.
For duty absolute how be fitter than now?
Or learn by shunning? Lord, I come; help thou.

TWENTY-THREE

Ever above my coldness and my doubt
Rises up something, reaching forth a band:
This thing I know, but cannot understand.
Is it the God in me that rises out

Beyond my self, trailing it up with him,
Towards the spirit-home, the freedom-land,
Beyond my conscious ken, my near horizon's brim?

TWENTY-FOUR

O God of man, my heart would worship all
My fellow men, the flashes from thy fire;
Them in good sooth my lofty kindred call,
Born of the same one heart, the perfect sire;
Love of my kind alone can set me free;
Help me to welcome all that come to me,
Not close my doors and dream solitude liberty!

TWENTY-FIVE

A loving word may set some door ajar
Where seemed no door, and that may enter in
Which lay at the heart of that same loving word
In my still chamber dwell thou always, Lord;
Thy presence there will carriage true afford;
True words will flow, pure of design to win;
And to my men my door shall have no bar.

TWENTY-SIX

My prayers, my God, flow from what I am not;
I think thy answers make me what I am.
Like weary waves thought follows upon thought,
But the still depth beneath is all thine own,
And there thou mov'st in paths to us unknown.
Out of strange strife thy peace is strangely wrought;
If the lion in us pray—thou answerest the lamb.

TWENTY-SEVEN

So bound in selfishness am I, so chained,
I know it must be glorious to be free
But know not what, full-fraught, the word doth mean.
By loss on loss I have severely gained

Wisdom enough my slavery to see;
But liberty, pure, absolute, serene,
No freest-visioned slave has ever seen.

TWENTY-EIGHT

For, that great freedom how should such as I
Be able to imagine in such a self?
Less hopeless far the miser man might try
To image the delight of friend-shared pelf.
Freedom is to be like thee, face and heart;
To know it, Lord, I must be as thou art,
I cannot breed the imagination high.

TWENTY-NINE

Yet hints come to me from the realm unknown;
Airs drift across the twilight border land,
Odored with life; and as from some far strand
Sea-murmured, whispers to my heart are blown
That fill me with a joy I cannot speak,
Yea, from whose shadow words drop faint and weak:
Thee, God, I shadow in that region grand.

THIRTY

O Christ, who didst appear in Judah land,
Thence by the cross go back to God's right hand,
Plain history, and things our sense beyond,
In thee together come and correspond:
How rulest thou from the undiscovered bourn
The world-wise world that laughs thee still to scorn?
Please, Lord, let thy disciple understand.

THIRTY-ONE

'Tis heart on heart thou rulest. Thou art the same
At God's right hand as here exposed to shame,
And therefore workest now as thou didst then—
Feeding the faint divine in humble men.

Through all thy realms from thee goes out heart-power,
Working the holy, satisfying hour,
When all shall love, and all be loved again.

JUNE

Up I would be to help thee—for thou liest
Not, linen-swathed in Joseph's garden tomb,
But walkest crowned, creation's heart and bloom.

June

One

FROM THINE, AS THEN, THE HEALING VIRTUE GOES
Into our hearts—that is the Father's plan.
From heart to heart it sinks, it steals, it flows,
From these that know thee still infecting those.
Here is my heart—from thine, Lord, fill it up,
That I may offer it as the holy cup
Of thy communion to my every man.

Two

When thou dost send out whirlwinds on thy seas,
Alternatest thy lightning with its roar,
Thy night with morning, and thy clouds with stars
Or, mightier force unseen in midst of these,
Orderest the life in every airy pore;
Guidest men's efforts, rul'st mishaps and jars—
'Tis only for their hearts, and nothing more.

Three

This, this alone thy Father careth for—
That men should live hearted throughout with thee—
Because the simple, only life thou art,
Of the very truth of living, the pure heart.

For this, deep waters whelm the fruitful lea,
Wars ravage, famine wastes, plague withers, nor
Shall cease till men have chosen the better part.

FOUR

But, like a virtuous medicine, self-diffused
Through all men's hearts thy love shall sink and float;
Till every feeling false, and thought unwise,
Selfish, and seeking, shall, sternly disused,
Wither, and die, and shrivel up to nought;
And Christ, whom they did hang 'twixt earth and skies,
Up in the inner world of men arise.

FIVE

Make me a fellow worker with thee, Christ;
Nought else befits a God-born energy;
Of all that's lovely, only lives the highest,
Lifing the rest that it shall never die.
Up I would be to help thee—for thou liest
Not, linen-swathed in Joseph's garden-tomb,
But walkest crowned, creation's heart and bloom.

SIX

My God, when I would lift my heart to thee,
Imagination instantly doth set
A cloudy something, thin, and vast, and vague,
To stand for him who is the fact of me;
Then up the will, and doth her weakness plague
To pay the heart her duty and her debt,
Showing the face that hearkeneth to the plea.

SEVEN

And hence it comes that thou at times dost scorn
To fade into an image of my mind;
I, dreamer, cover, hide thee up with dream—
Thee, primal, individual entity!

No likeness will I seek to frame or find,
But cry to that which thou dost choose to be,
To that which is my sight, therefore I cannot see.

EIGHT

No likeness? Lo, the Christ! Oh, large Enough!
I see, yet fathom not the face he wore.
He is—and out of him there is no stuff
To make a man. Let fail me every spark
Of blissful vision on my pathway rough,
I have seen much, and trust the perfect more,
While to his feet my faith crosses the wayless dark.

NINE

Faith is the human shadow of thy might.
Thou art the one self-perfect life, and we
Who trust thy life, therein join on to thee,
Taking our part in self-creating light.
To trust is to step forward out of the night—
To be—to share in the outgoing will
That lives and is, because outgoing still.

TEN

I am lost before thee Father! Yet I will
Claim of thee my birthright ineffable.
Thou lay'st it on me, son, to claim thee, sire;
To that which thou hast made me, I aspire;
To thee, the sun, upflames thy kindled fire.
No man presumes in that to which he was born;
Less than the gift to claim, would be the giver to scorn.

ELEVEN

Henceforth all things thy dealings are with me
For out of thee is nothing, or can be,
And all things are to draw us home to thee.
What matter that the knowers scoffing say,

"This is old folly, plain to the new day"?
If thou be such as thou, and they as they,
Unto thy *Let there be,* they still must answer *Nay.*

TWELVE

They will not, therefore cannot, do not know him.
Nothing they could know, could be God. In sooth,
Unto the true alone exists the truth.
They say well, saying nature doth not show him:
Truly she shows not what she cannot show;
And they deny the thing they cannot know.
Who sees a glory, towards it will go.

THIRTEEN

Faster no step moves God because the fool
Shouts to the universe God there is none;
The blindest man will not preach out the sun,
Though on his darkness he should found a school.
It may be, when he finds he is not dead,
Though world and body, sight and sound are fled,
Some eyes may open in his foolish head.

FOURTEEN

When I am very weary with hard thought,
And yet the question burns and is not quenched,
My heart grows cool when to remembrance wrought
That thou who know'st the light-born answer sought
Know'st too the dark where the doubt lies entrenched—
Know'st with what seemings I am sore perplexed,
And that with thee I wait, nor needs my soul be vexed.

FIFTEEN

Who sets himself not sternly to be good,
Is but a fool, who judgment of true things
Has none, however oft the claim renewed.
And he who thinks, in his great plenitude,

To right himself, and set his spirit free,
Without the might of higher communings,
Is foolish also—save he willed himself to be.

SIXTEEN

How many helps thou giv'st to those would learn!
To some sore pain, to others a sinking heart;
To some a weariness worse than any smart;
To some a haunting, fearing, blind concern;
Madness to some; to some the shaking dart
Of hideous death still following as they turn;
To some a hunger that will not depart.

SEVENTEEN

To some thou giv'st a deep unrest—a scorn
Of all they are or see upon the earth;
A gaze, at dusky night and clearing morn,
As on a land of emptiness and dearth;
To some a bitter sorrow; to some the sting
Of love misprized—of sick abandoning;
To some a frozen heart, oh, worse than anything!

EIGHTEEN

To some a mocking demon, that doth set
The poor foiled will to scoff at the ideal,
But loathsome makes to them their life of jar.
The messengers of Satan think to mar,
But make—driving the soul from false to feal—
To thee, the reconciler, the one real,
In whom alone the *would be* and the *is* are met.

NINETEEN

Me thou hast given an infinite unrest,
A hunger—not at first after known good,
But something vague I knew not, and yet would—
The veiled Isis, thy will not understood;

A conscience tossing ever in my breast;
And something deeper, that will not be expressed,
Save as the Spirit thinking in the Spirit's brood.

TWENTY

But now the Spirit and I are one in this—
My hunger now is after righteousness;
My spirit hopes in God to set me free
From the low self loathed of the higher me.
Great elder brother of my second birth,
Dear o'er all names but one, in heaven or earth,
Teach me all day to love eternally.

TWENTY-ONE

Lo, Lord, thou know'st, I would not anything
That in the heart of God holds not its root;
Nor falsely deem there is any life at all
That doth in him nor sleep nor shine nor sing;
I know the plants that bear the noisome fruit
Of burning and of ashes and of gall—
From God's heart torn, rootless to man's they cling.

TWENTY-TWO

Life-giving love rots to devouring fire;
Justice corrupts to despicable revenge;
Motherhood chokes in the dam's jealous mire;
Hunger for growth turns fluctuating change;
Love's anger grand grows spiteful human wrath.
Hunting men out of conscience' holy path;
And human kindness takes the tattler's range.

TWENTY-THREE

Nothing can draw the heart of man but good;
Low good it is that draws him from the higher—
So evil—poison uncreate from food.
Never a foul thing, with temptation dire,

Tempts hellward force created to aspire,
But walks in wronged strength of imprisoned truth,
Whose mantle also oft the shame indu'th.

TWENTY-FOUR

Love in the prime not yet I understand—
Scarce know the love that loveth at first hand:
Help me my selfishness to scatter and scout;
Blow on me till my love loves burningly;
Then the great love will burn the mean self out,
And I, in glorious simplicity,
Living by love, shall love unspeakably.

TWENTY-FIVE

Oh, make my anger pure—let no worst wrong
Rouse in me the old niggard selfishness.
Give me thine indignation—which is love
Turned on the evil that would part love's throng;
Thy anger scathes because it needs must bless,
Gathering into union calm and strong
All things on earth, and under, and above.

TWENTY-SIX

Make my forgiveness downright—such as I
Should perish if I did not have from thee;
I let the wrong go, withered up and dry,
Cursed with divine forgetfulness in me.
'Tis but self-pity, pleasant, mean, and sly,
Low whispering bids the paltry memory live:
What am I brother for, but to forgive!

TWENTY-SEVEN

"Thou art my father's child—come to my heart."
Thus must I say, or thou must say, "Depart";
Thus I would say—I would be as thou art;
Thus I must say, or still I work athwart

The absolute necessity and law
That dwells in me, and will me asunder draw,
If in obedience I leave any flaw.

TWENTY-EIGHT

Lord, I forgive—and step in unto thee.
If I have enemies, Christ deal with them:
He hath forgiven me and Jerusalem.
Lord, set me from self-inspiration free,
And let me live and think from thee, not me—
Rather, from deepest me then think and feel,
At center of thought's swift-revolving wheel.

TWENTY-NINE

I sit o'ercanopied with Beauty's tent,
Through which flies many a golden-winged dove,
Well watched of Fancy's tender eyes up bent;
A hundred Powers wait on me, ministering;
A thousand treasures Art and Knowledge bring;
Will, Conscience, Reason tower the rest above;
But in the midst, alone, I gladness am and love.

THIRTY

'Tis but a vision, Lord; I do not mean
That thus I am, or have one moment been—
'Tis but a picture hung upon my wall,
To measure dull contentment therewithal,
And know behind the human how I fall—
A vision true, of what one day shall be,
When thou hast had thy very will with me.

JULY

He builds me now—and if I cannot see
At anytime what he is doing with me,
'Tis that he makes the house for me too grand.

JULY

ONE

ALAS, MY TENT! SEE THROUGH IT A WHIRLWIND SWEEP!
Moaning, poor Fancy's doves are swept away.
I sit alone, a sorrow half asleep,
My consciousness the blackness all astir.
No pilgrim I, a homeless wanderer—
For how canst thou be in the darkness deep,
Who dwellest only in the living day?

TWO

It must be, somewhere in my fluttering tent,
Strange creatures, half tamed only yet, are pent—
Dragons, lop-winged birds, and large-eyed snakes!
Hark, through the storm the saddest howling breaks!
Or are they loose, roaming about the bent,
The darkness dire deepening with moan and scream?
My Morning, rise, and all shall be a dream.

THREE

Not thine, my Lord, the darkness all is mine
Save that, as mine, my darkness too is thine:
All things are thine to save or to destroy—
Destroy my darkness, rise my perfect joy;

Love primal, the live coal of every night,
Flame out, scare the ill things with radiant fright,
And fill my tent with laughing morn's delight.

FOUR

Master, thou workest with such common things—
Low souls, weak hearts, I mean—and hast to use,
Therefore, such common means and rescuings,
That hard we find it, as we sit and muse,
To think thou workest in us verily:
Bad sea-boats we, and manned with wretched crews—
That doubt the captain, watch the storm-spray flee.

FIVE

Thou art hampered in thy natural working then
When beings designed on freedom's holy plan
Will not be free: with thy poor, foolish men,
Thou therefore hast to work just like a man.
But when, tangling thyself in their sore need,
Thou hast to freedom fashioned them indeed,
Then wilt thou grandly move, and godlike speed.

SIX

Will this not then show grandest fact of all
In thy creation victory most renowned—
That thou hast wrought thy will by slow and small,
And made men like thee, though thy making bound
By that which they were not, and could not be
Until thou mad'st them make along with thee?
Master, the tardiness is but in me.

SEVEN

Hence come thy checks—because I still would run
My head into the sand, not flutter aloft
Towards thy home, with thy wind under me.
'Tis because I am mean, thy ways so oft

Look mean to me; my rise is low begun;
But scarce thy will doth grasp me, ere I see,
For my arrest and rise, its stern necessity.

EIGHT

Like clogs upon the pinions of thy plan
We hang—like captives on thy chariot-wheels,
Who should climb up and ride with Death's conqueror;
Therefore thy train along the world's highway steals
So slow to the peace of heart-reluctant man.
What shall we do to spread the wing and soar,
Nor straiten thy deliverance anymore?

NINE

The sole way to put flight into the wing,
To preen its feathers, and to make them grow,
Is to heed humbly every smallest thing
With which the Christ in us has aught to do.
So will the Christ from child to manhood go,
Obedient to the Father Christ, and so
Sweet holy change will turn all our old things to new.

TEN

Creation thou dost work by faint degrees,
By shade and shadow from unseen beginning;
Far, far apart, in unthought mysteries
Of thy own dark, unfathomable seas,
Thou will'st thy will; and thence, upon the earth—
Slow travelling, his way through centuries winning—
A child at length arrives at never ending birth.

ELEVEN

Well mayst thou then work on indocile hearts
By small successes, disappointments small;
By nature, weather, failure, or sore fall;
By shame, anxiety, bitterness, and smarts;

By loneliness, by weary loss of zest:
The rags, the husks, the swine, the hunger-quest,
Drive home the wanderer to the Father's breast!

TWELVE

How suddenly some rapid turn of thought
May throw the life-machine all out of gear,
Clouding the windows with the steam of doubt,
Filling the eyes with dust, with noise the ear!
Who knows not then where dwells the engineer,
Rushes aghast into the pathless night,
And wanders in a land of dreary fright.

THIRTEEN

Amazed at sightless whirring of their wheels
Confounded with the recklessness and strife,
Distract with fears of what may next ensue,
Some break rude exit from the house of life,
And plunge into a silence out of view—
Whence not a cry, no wafture once reveals
What door they have broke open with the knife.

FOURTEEN

Help me, my Father, in whatever dismay,
Whatever terror in whatever shape,
To hold the faster by thy garment's hem;
When my heart sinks, oh, lift it up, I pray;
Thy child should never fear though hell should gape,
Not blench though all the ills that men affray
Stood round him like the Romans round Jerusalem.

FIFTEEN

Too eager I must not be to understand.
How should the work the Master goes about
Fit the vague sketch my compasses have planned?
I am his house—for him to go in and out.

He builds me now—and if I cannot see
At anytime what he is doing with me,
'Tis that he makes the house for me too grand.

SIXTEEN

The house is not for me—it is for him.
His royal thoughts require many a stair,
Many a tower, many an outlook fair,
Of which I have no thought, and need no care.
Where I am most perplexed, it may be there
Thou mak'st a secret chamber, holy-dim,
Where thou wilt come to help my deepest prayer.

SEVENTEEN

I cannot tell why this day I am ill;
But I am well because it is thy will—
Which is to make me pure and right like thee.
Not yet I need escape—'tis bearable
Because thou knowest. And when harder things
Shall rise and gather, and overshadow me,
I shall have comfort in thy strengthenings.

EIGHTEEN

How do I live when thou art far away?
When I am sunk, and lost, and dead in sleep,
Or in some dream with no sense in its play?
When weary-dull, or drowned in study deep?
O Lord, I live so utterly on thee,
I live when I forget thee utterly—
Not that thou thinkest of, but thinkest me.

NINETEEN

Thou far! That word the holy truth doth blur.
Doth the great ocean from the small fish run
When it sleeps fast in its low weedy bower?
Is the sun far from any smallest flower,

That lives by his dear presence every hour?
Are they not one in oneness without stir—
The flower the flower because the sun the sun?

TWENTY

"Dear presence every hour"! What of the night,
When crumpled daisies shut gold sadness in;
And some do hang the head for lack of light,
Sick almost unto death with absence-blight?
Thy memory then, warm-lingering in the ground,
Mourned dewy in the air, keeps their hearts sound,
Till fresh with day their lapsed life begin.

TWENTY-ONE

All things are shadows of the shining true:
Sun, sea, and air—close, potent, hurtless fire—
Flowers from their mother's prison—dove, and dew—
Everything holds a slender guiding clue
Back to the mighty oneness: hearts of faith
Know thee than light, than heat, endlessly nigher,
Our life's life, carpenter of Nazareth.

TWENTY-TWO

Sometimes, perhaps, the spiritual blood runs slow,
And soft along the veins of will doth flow,
Seeking God's arteries from which it came.
Or does the ethereal, creative flame
Turn back upon itself, and latent grow?
It matters not what figure or what name,
If thou art in me, and I am not to blame.

TWENTY-THREE

In such God-silence, the soul's nest, so long
As all is still, no flutter and no song,
Is safe. But if my soul begin to act
Without some waking to the eternal fact

That my dear life is hid with Christ in God—
I think and move a creature of earth's clod,
Stand on the finite, act upon the wrong.

TWENTY-FOUR

My soul this sermon hence for itself prepares:
"Then is there nothing vile thou mayst not do,
Buffeted in a tumult of low cares,
And treacheries of the old man 'gainst the new."
Lord, in my spirit let thy Spirit move,
Warning, that it may not have to reprove—
In my dead moments, Master, stir the prayers.

TWENTY-FIVE

Lord, let my soul o'erburdened then feel thee
Thrilling through all its brain's stupidity.
If I must slumber, heedless of ill harms,
Let it not be but in my Father's arms;
Outside the shelter of his garment's fold,
All is a waste, a terror-haunted wold.
Lord, keep me. 'Tis thy child that cries. Behold.

TWENTY-SIX

Some say that thou their endless love hast won
By deeds for them which I may not believe
Thou ever didst, or ever willedst done:
What matter, so they love thee? They receive
Eternal more than the poor loom and wheel
Of their invention ever wove and spun.
I love thee for I must, thine all from head to heel.

TWENTY-SEVEN

The love of thee will set all notions right.
Right save by love no thought can be or may;
Only love's knowledge is the primal light.
Questions keep camp along love's shining coast—

Challenge my love and would my entrance stay:
Across the buzzing, doubting, challenging host,
I rush to thee, and cling, and cry: *Thou know'st.*

TWENTY-EIGHT

Oh, let me live in thy realities,
Nor substitute my notions for thy facts,
Notion with notion making leagues and pacts;
They are to truth but as dream-deeds to acts,
And questioned, make me doubt of everything.
"O Lord, my God," my heart gets up and cries,
"Come thy own self, and with thee my faith bring."

TWENTY-NINE

O Master, my desires to work, to know,
To be aware that I do live and grow—
All restless wish for anything not thee,
I yield, and on thy altar offer me.
Let me no more from out thy presence go,
But keep me waiting watchful for thy will—
Even while I do it, waiting watchful still.

THIRTY

Thou art the Lord of life, the secret thing.
Thou wilt give endless more than I could find,
Even if without thee I could go and seek;
For thou art one, Christ, with my deepest mind
Duty alive, self-willed, in me doth speak,
And to a deeper purer being sting:
I come to thee, my life, my causing kind.

THIRTY-ONE

Nothing is alien in thy world immense—
No look of sky or earth or man or beast;
"In the great hand of God I stand, and thence"
Look out on life, his endless, holy feast.

To try to feel is but to court despair,
To dig for a sun within a garden-fence:
Who does thy will, O God, he lives upon thy air.

AUGUST

The holiest bread, if hoarded, soon will breed
The mammon-moth, the having-pride, I find.
'Tis momently thy heart gives out heart-quickening.

AUGUST

ONE

SO SHALL ABUNDANT ENTRANCE ME BE GIVEN
Into the truth, my life's inheritance.
Lo, as the sun shoots straight from out his tomb,
God-floated, casting round a lordly glance
Into the corners of his endless room,
So, through the rent which thou, O Christ, hast riven,
I enter liberty's divine expanse.

TWO

It will be so—ah, so it is not now!
Who seeks thee for a little lazy peace,
Then, like a man all weary of the plow,
That leaves it standing in the furrow's crease,
Turns from thy presence for a foolish while,
Till comes again the rasp of unrest's file,
From liberty is distant many a mile.

THREE

Like one that stops, and drinks, and turns, and goes
Into a land where never water flows,
There travels on, the dry and thirsty day,
Until the hot night veils the farther way,

Then turns and finds again the bubbling pool—
Here would I build my house, take up my stay,
Nor ever leave my Sychar's margin cool.

FOUR

Keep me, Lord, with thee. I call from out the dark—
Hear in thy light, of which I am a spark.
I know not what is mine and what is thine—
Of branch and stem I miss the differing mark—
But if a mere hair's-breadth me separateth,
That hair's-breadth is eternal, infinite death.
For sap thy dead branch calls, O living Vine!

FIVE

I have no choice, I must do what I can;
But thou dost me, and all things else as well;
Thou wilt take care thy child shall grow a man.
Rouse thee, my faith; be king; with life be one;
To trust in God is action's highest kind;
Who trusts in God, his heart with life doth swell;
Faith opens all the windows to God's wind.

SIX

O Father, thou art my eternity.
Not on the clasp of consciousness—on thee
My life depends; and I can well afford
All to forget, so thou remember, Lord.
In thee I rest; in sleep thou dost me fold;
In thee I labor; still in thee, grow old;
And dying, shall I not in thee, my Life, be bold?

SEVEN

In holy things may be unholy greed.
Thou giv'st a glimpse of many a lovely thing,
Not to be stored for use in any mind,
But only for the present spiritual need.

The holiest bread, if hoarded, soon will breed
The mammon-moth, the having-pride, I find.
'Tis momently thy heart gives out heart-quickening.

EIGHT

It is thyself, and neither this nor that,
Nor anything, told, taught, or dreamed of thee,
That keeps us live. The holy maid who sat
Low at thy feet, choosing the better part,
Rising, bore with her—what a memory!
Yet, brooding only on that treasure, she
Had soon been roused by conscious loss of heart.

NINE

I am a fool when I would stop and think,
And lest I lose my thoughts, from duty shrink.
It is but avarice in another shape.
'Tis as the vine-branch were to hoard the grape,
Nor trust the living root beneath the sod.
What trouble is that child to thee, my God,
Who sips thy gracious cup, and will not drink!

TEN

True, faithful action only is the life,
The grapes for which we feel the pruning knife.
Thoughts are but leaves; they fall and feed the ground.
The holy seasons, swift and slow, go round;
The ministering leaves return, fresh, large, and rife—
But fresher, larger, more thoughts to the brain—
Farewell, my dove! Come back, hope-laden, through the rain.

ELEVEN

Well may this body poorer, feebler grow!
It is undressing for its last sweet bed;
But why should the soul, which death shall never know,
Authority, and power, and memory shed?

It is that love with absolute faith would wed;
God takes the inmost garments off his child,
To have him in his arms, naked and undefiled.

TWELVE

Thou art my knowledge and my memory,
No less than my real, deeper life, my love.
I will not fool, degrade myself to trust
In less than that which maketh me say *Me,*
In less than that causing itself to be.
Thou art within me, behind, beneath, above—
I will be thine because I may and must.

THIRTEEN

Thou art the truth, the life. Thou, Lord, wilt see
To every question that perplexes me.
I am thy being; and my dignity
Is written with my name down in thy book;
Thou wilt care for it. Never shall I think
Of anything that thou mightest overlook—
In faith-born triumph at thy feet I sink.

FOURTEEN

Thou carest more for that which I call mine,
In same sort—better manner than I could,
Even if I knew creation's ends divine,
Rousing in me this vague desire of good.
Thou art more to me than my desires' whole brood;
Thou art the only person, and I cry
Unto the Father *I* of this my *I.*

FIFTEEN

Thou who inspirest prayer, then bend'st thine ear;
Its crying with love's grand respect to hear!
I cannot give myself to thee aright—
With the triumphant uttermost of gift;

That cannot be till I am full of light—
To perfect deed a perfect will must lift:
Inspire, possess, compel me, first of every might.

SIXTEEN

I do not wonder men can ill believe
Who make poor claims upon thee, perfect Lord;
Then most I trust when most I would receive.
I wonder not that such do pray and grieve—
The God they think, to be God is not fit.
Then only in thy glory I seem to sit,
When my heart claims from thine an infinite accord.

SEVENTEEN

More life I need ere I myself can be.
Sometimes, when the eternal tide ebbs low,
A moment weary of my life I grow—
Weary of my existence' self, I mean,
Not of its plodding, not its wind and snow
Then to thy knee trusting I turn, and lean:
Thou will'st I live, and I do will with thee.

EIGHTEEN

Dost thou mean sometimes that we should forget thee,
Dropping the veil of things 'twixt thee and us?
Ah, not that we should lose thee and regret thee!
But that, we turning from our windows thus,
The frost-fixed God should vanish from the pane,
Sun-melted, and a moment, Father, let thee
Look like thyself straight into heart and brain.

NINETEEN

For sometimes when I am busy among men,
With heart and brain an open thoroughfare
For faces, words, and thoughts other than mine,
And a pause comes at length—oh, sudden then,

Back throbs the tide with rush exultant rare;
And for a gentle moment I divine
Thy dawning presence flush my tremulous air.

TWENTY

If I have to forget thee, do thou see
It be a good, not bad forgetfulness;
That all its mellow, truthful air be free
From dusty *noes,* and soft with many a *yes;*
That as thy breath my life, my life may be
Man's breath. So when thou com'st at hour unknown,
Thou shalt find nothing in me but thine own.

TWENTY-ONE

Thou being in me, in my deepest me,
Through all the time I do not think of thee,
Shall I not grow at last so true within
As to forget thee and yet never sin?
Shall I not walk the loud world's busy way,
Yet in thy palace-porch sit all the day?
Not conscious think of thee, yet never from thee stray?

TWENTY-TWO

Forget! Oh, must it be? Would it were rather
That every sense was so filled with my Father
That not in anything could I forget him,
But deepest, highest must in all things set him!
Yet if thou think in me, God, what great matter
Though my poor thought to former break and latter—
As now my best thoughts break, before thee foiled, and scatter!

TWENTY-THREE

Some way there must be of my not forgetting,
And thither thou art leading me, my God.
The child that, weary of his mother's petting,
Runs out the moment that his feet are shod,

May see her face in every flower he sees,
And she, although beyond the window sitting,
Be nearer him than when he sat upon her knees.

TWENTY-FOUR

What if, when I at last, at the long last,
Shall see thy face, my Lord, my life's delight,
It should not be the face that hath been glassed
In poor imagination's mirror slight!
Will my soul sink, and shall I stand aghast,
Beggared of hope, my heart a conscious blight,
Amazed and lost—death's bitterness come and not passed?

TWENTY-FIVE

Ah, no! For from thy heart the love will press,
And shining from thy perfect human face,
Will sink into me like the father's kiss;
And deepening wide the gulf of consciousness
Beyond imagination's lowest abyss,
Will, with the potency of creative grace,
Lord it throughout the larger thinking place.

TWENTY-SIX

Thus God-possessed, new born, ah, not for long
Should I the sight behold, beatified,
Know it creating in me, feel the throng
Of speechless hopes out-throbbing like a tide.
And my heart rushing, borne aloft the flood,
To offer at his feet its living blood—
Ere, glory-hid, the other face I spied.

TWENTY-SEVEN

For our imagination is, in small,
And with the making-difference that must be,
Mirror of God's creating mirror; all
That shows itself therein, that formeth he,

And there is Christ, no bodiless vanity,
Though, face to face, the mighty perfectness
With glory blurs the dim-reflected less.

TWENTY-EIGHT

I clasp thy feet, O Father of the living!
Thou wilt not let my fluttering hopes be more,
Or lovelier, or greater, than thy giving!
Surely thy ships will bring to my poor shore,
Of gold and peacocks such a shining store
As will laugh all the dreams to holy scorn,
Of love and sorrow that were ever born.

TWENTY-NINE

Sometimes it seems pure natural to trust,
And trust right largely, grandly, infinitely,
Daring the splendor of the giver's part;
At other times, the whole earth is but dust,
The sky is dust, yea, dust the human heart;
Then art thou nowhere, there is no room for thee
In the great dust-heap of eternity.

THIRTY

But why should it be possible to mistrust—
Nor possible only, but its opposite hard?
Why should not man believe because he must—
By sight's compulsion? Why should he be scarred
With conflict? Worn with doubting fine and long?
No man is fit for heaven's musician throng
Who has not tuned an instrument all shook and jarred.

THIRTY-ONE

Therefore, O Lord, when all things common seem,
When all is dust, and self the center clod,
When grandeur is a hopeless, foolish dream,
And anxious care more reasonable than God—

Out of the ashes I will call to thee—
In spite of dead distrust call earnestly:
O thou who livest, call, then answer dying me.

SEPTEMBER

Yet more and more of me thou dost demand;
My faith and hope in God alone shall stand,
The life of law—not trust the rain and sun
To draw the golden harvest o'er the land.

September

One

WE ARE A SHADOW AND A SHINING, WE!
One moment nothing seems but what we see,
Nor aught to rule but common circumstance—
Nought is to seek but praise, to shun but chance;
A moment more, and God is all in all,
And not a sparrow from its nest can fall
But from the ground its chirp goes up into his hall.

Two

I know at least which is the better mood.
When on a heap of cares I sit and brood,
Like Job upon his ashes, sorely vext,
I feel a lower thing than when I stood
The world's true heir, fearless as, on its stalk,
A lily meeting Jesus in his walk:
I am not all mood—I can judge betwixt.

Three

Such differing moods can scarce to one belong;
Shall the same fountain sweet and bitter yield?
Shall what bore late the dust-mood, think and brood
Till it bring forth the great believing mood?

Or that which bore the grand mood, bald and peeled,
Sit down to croon the shabby sensual song,
To hug itself, and sink from wrong to meaner wrong?

FOUR

In the low mood, the mere man acts alone,
Moved by impulses which, if from within,
Yet far outside the center man begin;
But in the grand mood, every softest tone
Comes from the living God at very heart—
From thee who infinite core of being art,
Thee who didst call our names ere ever we could sin.

FIVE

There is a coward sparing in the heart,
Offspring of penury and low-born fear—
Prayer must take heed nor overdo its part,
Asking too much of him with open ear!
Sinners must wait, not seek the very best,
Cry out for peace, and be of middling cheer—
False heart, thou cheatest God, and dost thy life molest.

SIX

Thou hungerest not, thou thirstest not enough.
Thou art a temporizing thing, mean heart.
Down-drawn, thou pick'st up straws and wretched stuff,
Stooping as if the world's floor were the chart
Of the long way thy lazy feet must tread.
Thou dreamest of the crown hung o'er thy head—
But that is safe—thou gatherest hairs and fluff!

SEVEN

Man's highest action is to reach up higher,
Stir up himself to take hold of his sire.
Then best I love you, dearest, when I go
And cry to love's life I may love you so

As to content the yearning, making love,
That perfects strength divine in weakness' fire,
And from the broken pots calls out the silver dove.

EIGHT

Poor am I, God knows, poor as withered leaf;
Poorer or richer than, I dare not ask.
To love aright, for me were hopeless task,
Eternities too high to comprehend.
But shall I tear my heart in hopeless grief,
Or rise and climb, and run and kneel, and bend,
And drink the primal love—so love in chief?

NINE

Then love shall wake and be its own high life.
Then shall I know 'tis I that love indeed—
Ready, without a moment's questioning strife,
To be forgot, like bursting water-bead,
For the high good of the eternal dear;
All hope, all claim, resting, with spirit clear,
Upon the living love that every love doth breed.

TEN

Ever I seem to fail in utterance.
Sometimes amid the swift melodious dance
Of fluttering words—as if it had not been,
The thought has melted, vanished into night;
Sometimes I say a thing I did not mean,
And lo, 'tis better, by thy ordered chance,
Than what eluded me, floating too feathery light.

ELEVEN

If thou wouldst have me speak, Lord, give me speech,
So many cries are uttered now-a-days,
That scarce a song, however clear and true,
Will thread the jostling tumult safe, and reach

The ears of men buz-filled with poor denays:
Barb thou my words with light, make my song new,
And men will hear, or when I sing or preach.

TWELVE

Can anything go wrong with me? I ask—
And the same moment, at a sudden pain,
Stand trembling. Up from the great river's brim
Comes a cold breath; the farther bank is dim;
The heaven is black with clouds and coming rain;
High soaring faith is grown a heavy task,
And all is wrong with weary heart and brain.

THIRTEEN

"Things do go wrong. I know grief, pain, and fear.
I see them lord it sore and wide around."
From her fair twilight answers Truth, star-crowned,
"Things wrong are needful where wrong things abound.
Things go not wrong; but Pain, with dog and spear,
False faith from human hearts will hunt and hound.
The earth shall quake 'neath them that trust the solid ground."

FOURTEEN

Things go not wrong when sudden I fall prone,
But when I snatch my upheld hand from thine,
And, proud or careless, think to walk alone.
Then things go wrong, when I, poor, silly sheep,
To shelves and pits from the good pasture creep;
Not when the shepherd leaves the ninety and nine,
And to the mountains goes, after the foolish one.

FIFTEEN

Lo, now thy swift dogs, over stone and bush,
After me, straying sheep, loud barking, rush.
There's *Fear,* and *Shame,* and *Empty-heart,* and *Lack,*
And *Lost-love,* and a thousand at their back!

I see thee not, but know thou hound'st them on,
And I am lost indeed—escape is none.
See, there they come, down streaming on my track!

SIXTEEN

I rise and run, staggering—double and run.
But whither—whither—whither for escape?
The sea lies all about this long-necked cape—
There come the dogs, straight for me everyone—
Me, live despair, live center of alarms!
Ah, lo, 'twixt me and all his barking harms,
The shepherd, lo, I run—fall folded in his arms.

SEVENTEEN

There let the dogs yelp, let them growl and leap;
It is no matter—I will go to sleep.
Like a spent cloud pass pain and grief and fear,
Out from behind it unchanged love shines clear.
Oh, save me, Christ! I know not what I am,
I was thy stupid, self-willed, greedy lamb,
Would be thy honest and obedient sheep.

EIGHTEEN

Why is it that so often I return
From social converse with a spirit worn,
A lack, a disappointment—even a sting
Of shame, as for some low, unworthy thing?
Because I have not, careful, first of all,
Set my door wide open, back to the wall,
Ere I at others' doors did knock and call.

NINETEEN

Yet more and more of me thou dost demand;
My faith and hope in God alone shall stand,
The life of law—not trust the rain and sun
To draw the golden harvest o'er the land.

I must not say: "This too will pass and die,"
"The wind will change," "Round will the seasons run."
Law is the body of will, of conscious harmony.

TWENTY

Who trusts a law, might worship a god of wood;
Half his soul slumbers, if it be not dead.
He is a live thing shut in chaos crude,
Hemmed in with dragons—a remorseless head
Still hanging over its uplifted eyes.
No; God is all in all, and nowhere dies—
The present heart and thinking will of good.

TWENTY-ONE

Law is our schoolmaster. Our Master, Christ,
Lived under all our laws, yet always prayed—
So walked the water when the storm was highest.
Law is thy Father's; thou hast it obeyed,
And it thereby subject to thee hast made—
To rule it, Master, for thy brethren's sakes—
Well may he guide the law by whom law's maker makes.

TWENTY-TWO

Death haunts our souls with dissolution's strife;
Soaks them with unrest; makes our every breath
A throe, not action; from God's purest gift
Wipes off the bloom; and on the harp of faith
Its fretted strings doth slacken still and shift:
Life everywhere, perfect, and always life,
Is sole redemption from this haunting death.

TWENTY-THREE

God, thou from death dost lift me. As I rise,
Its Lethe from my garment drips and flows.
Ere long I shall be safe in upper air,
With thee, my life—with thee, my answered prayer

Where thou art God in every wind that blows,
And self alone, and ever, softly dies,
There shall my being blossom, and I know.

TWENTY-FOUR

I would dig, Master, in no field but thine,
Would build my house only upon thy rock,
Yet am but a dull day, with a sea-sheen!
Why should I wonder then that they should mock,
Who, in the limbo of things heard and seen,
Hither and thither blowing, lose the shine
Of every light that hangs in the firmament divine.

TWENTY-FIVE

Lord, loosen in me the hold of visible things;
Help me to walk by faith and not by sight;
I would, through thickest veils and coverings,
See into the chambers of the living light.
Lord, in the land of things that swell and seem,
Help me to walk by the other light supreme,
Which shows thy facts behind man's vaguely hinting dream.

TWENTY-SIX

I see a little child whose eager hands
Search the thick stream that drains the crowded street
For possible things hid in its current slow.
Near by, behind him, a great palace stands,
Where kings might welcome nobles to their feet.
Soft sounds, sweet scents, fair sights there only go—
There the child's father lives, but the child does not know.

TWENTY-SEVEN

On, eager, hungry, busy-seeing child,
Rise up, turn round, run in, run up the stair.
Far in a chamber from rude noise exiled,
Thy father sits, pondering how thou dost fare.

The mighty man will clasp thee to his breast:
Will kiss thee, stroke the tangles of thy hair,
And lap thee warm in fold on fold of lovely rest.

TWENTY-EIGHT

The prince of this world came, and nothing found
In thee, O Master; but, ah, woe is me!
He cannot pass me, on other business bound,
But, spying in me things familiar, he
Casts over me the shadow of his flight,
And straight I moan in darkness—and the fight
Begins afresh betwixt the world and thee.

TWENTY-NINE

In my own heart, O Master, in my thought,
Betwixt the woolly sheep and hairy goat
Not clearly I distinguish; but I think
Thou knowest that I fight upon thy side.
The *how* I am ashamed of; for I shrink
From many a blow—am home on the battle-tide,
When I should rush to the front, and take thy foe by the throat.

THIRTY

The enemy still hath many things in me;
Yea, many an evil nest with open hole
Gapes out to him, at which he enters free.
But, like the impact of a burning coal,
His presence mere straight rouses the garrison,
And all are up in arms, and down on knee,
Fighting and praying till the foe is gone.

OCTOBER

The chips in me, the stones, the straws, the sand,
Cast them out with fine separating hand,
And make a vessel of thy yielding clay.

OCTOBER

ONE

Remember, Lord, thou hast not made me good.
Or if thou didst, it was so long ago
I have forgotten—and never understood,
I humbly think. At best it was a crude,
A rough-hewn goodness, that did need this woe,
This sin, these harms of all kinds fierce and rude.
To shape it out, making it live and grow.

TWO

But thou art making me, I thank thee, sire.
What thou hast done and doest thou know'st well,
And I will help thee: gently in thy fire
I will lie burning; on thy potter's-wheel
I will whirl patient, though my brain should reel.
Thy grace shall be enough the grief to quell,
And growing strength perfect through weakness dire.

THREE

I have not knowledge, wisdom, insight, thought,
Nor understanding, fit to justify
Thee in thy work, O Perfect. Thou hast brought
Me up to this—and, lo, what thou hast wrought,

I cannot call it good. But I can cry—
"O enemy, the maker hath not done;
One day thou shalt behold, and from the sight wilt run."

FOUR

The faith I win, aside is easily bent;
But of thy love, my God, one glimpse alone
Can make me absolutely confident—
With faith, hope, joy, in love responsive blent.
My soul then, in the vision mighty grown,
Its father and its fate securely known,
Falls on thy bosom with exultant moan.

FIVE

Thou workest perfectly. And if it seem
Some things are not so well, 'tis but because
They are too loving-deep, too lofty-wise,
For me, poor child, to understand their laws:
My highest wisdom half is but a dream;
My love runs helpless like a falling stream:
Thy good embraces ill, and lo, its illness dies!

SIX

From sleep I wake, and wake to think of thee.
But wherefore not with sudden glorious glee?
Why burst not gracious on me heaven and earth
In all the splendor of a new-day-birth?
Why hangs a cloud betwixt my Lord and me?
The moment that my eyes the morning greet,
My soul should panting rush to clasp thy father-feet.

SEVEN

Is it because it is not thou I see,
But only my poor, blotted fancy of thee?
Oh, never till thyself reveal thy face,
Shall I be flooded with life's vital grace.

Oh, make my mirror-heart thy shining-place,
And then my soul, awaking with the morn,
Shall be a waking joy, eternally new-born.

EIGHT

Lord, in my silver is much metal base,
Else should my being by this time have shown
Thee thy own self therein. Therefore do I
Wake in the furnace. I know thou sittest by,
Refining—look, keep looking in to try
Thy silver; Master, look and see thy face,
Else here I lie forever, blank as any stone.

NINE

But when in the dim silver thou dost look,
I do behold thy face, though blurred and faint.
O joy, no flaw in me thy grace will brook,
But still refine: slow shall the silver pass
From bright to brighter, till, sans spot or taint,
Love, well content, shall see no speck of brass,
And I his perfect face shall hold as in a glass.

TEN

With every morn my life afresh must break
The crust of self, gathered about me fresh;
That thy wind-spirit may rush in and shake
The darkness out of me, and rend the mesh
The spider-devils spin out of the flesh—
Eager to net the soul before it wake,
That it may slumberous lie, and listen to the snake.

ELEVEN

'Tis that I am not good—that is enough;
I pry no farther—that is not the way.
Here, O my potter, is thy making stuff!
Set thy wheel going; let it whir and play.

The chips in me, the stones, the straws, the sand,
Cast them out with fine separating hand,
And make a vessel of thy yielding clay.

TWELVE

What if it take a thousand years to make me,
So me he leave not, angry, on the floor!
Nay, thou art never angry—that would break me!
Would I tried never thy dear patience sore,
But were as good as thou couldst well expect me,
Whilst thou dost make, I mar, and thou correct me!
Then were I now content, waiting for something more.

THIRTEEN

Only, my God, see thou that I content thee—
Oh, take thy own content upon me, God!
Ah, never, never, sure, wilt thou repent thee,
That thou hast called thy Adam from the clod!
Yet must I mourn that thou shouldst ever find me
One moment sluggish, needing more of the rod
Than thou didst think when thy desire designed me.

FOURTEEN

My God, it troubles me I am not better.
More help, I pray, still more. Thy perfect debtor
I shall be when thy perfect child I am grown.
My Father, help me—am I not thine own?
Lo, other lords have had dominion o'er me,
But now thy will alone I set before me:
Thy own heart's life—Lord, thou wilt not abhor me!

FIFTEEN

In youth, when once again I had set out
To find thee, Lord, my life, my liberty,
A window now and then, clouds all about,
Would open into heaven: my heart forlorn

First all would tremble with a solemn glee,
Then, whelmed in peace, rest like a man outworn,
That sees the dawn slow part the closed lids of the morn.

SIXTEEN

Now I grow old, and the soft-gathered years
Have calmed, yea dulled the heart's swift fluttering beat;
But a quiet hope that keeps its household seat
Is better than recurrent glories fleet.
To know thee, Lord, is worth a many tears;
And when this mildew, age, has dried away,
My heart will beat again as young and strong and gay.

SEVENTEEN

Stronger and gayer tenfold! But, O friends,
Not for itself, nor any hoarded bliss.
I see but vaguely whither my being tends,
All vaguely spy a glory shadow-blent,
Vaguely desire the "individual kiss";
But when I think of God, a large content
Fills the dull air of my gray cloudy tent.

EIGHTEEN

Father of me, thou art my bliss secure.
Make of me, Maker, whatsoe'er thou wilt.
Let fancy's wings hang moulting, hope grow poor,
And doubt steam up from where a joy was spilt—
I lose no time to reason it plain and clear,
But fly to thee, my life's perfection dear:
Not what I think, but what thou art, makes sure.

NINETEEN

This utterance of spirit through still thought,
This forming of heart-stuff in molds of brain,
Is helpful to the soul by which 'tis wrought,
The shape reacting on the heart again;

But when I am quite old, and words are slow,
Like dying things that keep their holes for woe,
And memory's withering tendrils clasp with effort vain?

TWENTY

Thou, then as now, no less wilt be my life,
And I shall know it better than before,
Praying and trusting, hoping, claiming more.
From effort vain, sick foil, and bootless strife,
I shall, with childness fresh, look up to thee;
Thou, seeing thy child with age encumbered sore,
Wilt round him bend thine arm more carefully.

TWENTY-ONE

And when grim Death doth take me by the throat,
Thou wilt have pity on thy handiwork;
Thou wilt not let him on my suffering gloat,
But draw my soul out—gladder than man or boy,
When thy saved creatures from the narrow ark
Rushed out, and leaped and laughed and cried for joy,
And the great rainbow strode across the dark.

TWENTY-TWO

Against my fears, my doubts, my ignorance,
I trust in thee, O Father of my Lord!
The world went on in this same broken dance,
When, worn and mocked, he trusted and adored:
I too will trust, and gather my poor best
To face the truth-faced false. So in his nest
I shall awake at length, a little scarred and scored.

TWENTY-THREE

Things cannot look all right so long as I
Am not all right who see—therefore not right
Can see. The lamp within sends out the light
Which shows the things; and if its rays go wry,

Or are not white, they must part show a lie.
The man, half-cured, did men not trees conclude,
Because he moving saw what else had seemed a wood.

TWENTY-FOUR

Give me, take from me, as thou wilt. I learn—
Slowly and stubbornly I learn to yield
With a strange hopefulness. As from the field
Of hard-fought battle won, the victor chief
Turns thankfully, although his heart to yearn,
So from my old things to thy new I turn,
With sad, thee-trusting heart, and not in grief.

TWENTY-FIVE

If with my father I did wander free,
Floating o'er hill and field where'er we would,
And, lighting on the sward before the door,
Strange faces through the window-panes should see,
And strange feet standing where the loved had stood,
The dear old place theirs all, as ours before—
Should I be sorrowful, father, having thee?

TWENTY-SIX

So, Lord, if thou tak'st from me all the rest,
Thyself with each resumption drawing nigher,
It shall but hurt me as the thorn of the briar,
When I reach to the pale flower in its breast.
To have thee, Lord, is to have all thy best,
Holding it by its very life divine—
To let my friend's hand go, and take his heart in mine.

TWENTY-SEVEN

Take from me leisure, all familiar places;
Take all the lovely things of earth and air;
Take from me books; take all my precious faces;
Take words melodious, and their songful linking;

Take scents, and sounds, and all thy outsides fair;
Draw nearer, taking, and, to my sober thinking,
Thou bring'st them nearer all, and ready to my prayer.

TWENTY-EIGHT

No place on earth henceforth I shall count strange,
For every place belongeth to my Christ.
I will go calm where'er thou bid'st me range;
Whoe'er my neighbor, thou art still my nighest.
Oh, my heart's life, my owner, will of my being!
Into my soul thou every moment diest,
In thee my life thus evermore decreeing.

TWENTY-NINE

What though things change and pass, nor come again!
Thou, the life-heart of all things, changest never.
The sun shines on; the fair clouds turn to rain,
And glad the earth with many a spring and river.
The hearts that answer change with chill and shiver,
That mourn the past, sad-sick, with hopeless pain,
They know not thee, our changeless heart and brain.

THIRTY

My halting words will someday turn to song—
Some far-off day, in holy other times!
The melody now prisoned in my rimes
Will one day break aloft, and from the throng
Of wrestling thoughts and words spring up the air;
As from the flower its color's sweet despair
Issues in odor, and the sky's low levels climbs.

THIRTY-ONE

My surgent thought shoots lark-like up to thee.
Thou like the heaven art all about the lark.
Whatever I surmise or know in me,
Idea, or but symbol on the dark,

Is living, working, thought-creating power
In thee, the timeless Father of the hour.
I am thy book, thy song—thy child would be.

NOVEMBER

. . . when the children had made sparrows of clay,
Thou mad'st them birds, with wings to flutter and fold:
Take, Lord, my prayer in thy hand, and make it pray.

November

One

THOU ART OF THIS WORLD, CHRIST. THOU KNOW'ST IT ALL;
Thou know'st our evens, our morns, our red and gray;
How moons, and hearts, and seasons rise and fall;
How we grow weary plodding on the way;
Of future joy how present pain bereaves,
Rounding us with a dark of mere decay,
Tossed with a drift of summer-fallen leaves.

Two

Thou knowest all our weeping, fainting, striving;
Thou know'st how very hard it is *to be;*
How hard to rouse faint will not yet reviving;
To do the pure thing, trusting all to thee;
To hold thou art there, for all no face we see;
How hard to think, through cold and dark and dearth,
That thou art nearer now than when eye-seen on earth.

Three

Have pity on us for the look of things,
When blank denial stares us in the face.
Although the serpent mask have lied before,
It fascinates the bird that darkling sings,

And numbs the little prayer-bird's beating wings.
For how believe thee somewhere in blank space,
If through the darkness come no knocking to our door?

FOUR

If we might sit until the darkness go,
Possess our souls in patience perhaps we might;
But there is always something to be done,
And no heart left to do it. To and fro
The dull thought surges, as the driven waves fight
In gulfy channels. O victorious one,
Give strength to rise, go out, and meet thee in the night.

FIVE

"Wake, thou that sleepest; rise up from the dead,
And Christ will give thee light." I do not know
What sleep is, what is death, or what is light;
But I am waked enough to feel a woe,
To rise and leave death. Stumbling through the night,
To my dim lattice, O calling Christ, I go,
And out into the dark look for thy star-crowned head.

SIX

There are who come to me, and write, and send,
Whom I would love, giving good things to all,
But *friend*—that name I cannot on them spend;
'Tis from the center of self-love they call
For cherishing—for which they first must know
How to be still, and take the seat that's low:
When, Lord, shall I be fit—when wilt thou call me friend?

SEVEN

Wilt thou not one day, Lord? In all my wrong,
Self-love and weakness, laziness and fear,
This one thing I can say: *I am content*
To be and have what in thy heart I am meant

To be and have. In my best times I long
After thy will, and think it glorious-dear;
Even in my worst, perforce my will to thine is bent.

EIGHT

My God, I look to thee for tenderness
Such as I could not seek from any man,
Or in a human heart fancy or plan—
A something deepest prayer will not express:
Lord, with thy breath blow on my being's fires,
Until, even to the soul with self-love wan,
I yield the primal love, that no return desires.

NINE

Only no word of mine must ever foster
The self that in a brother's bosom gnaws;
I may not fondle failing, nor the boaster
Encourage with the breath of my applause.
Weakness needs pity, sometimes love's rebuke:
Strength only sympathy deserves and draws—
And grows by every faithful loving look.

TEN

'Tis but as men draw nigh to thee, my Lord,
They can draw nigh each other and not hurt.
Who with the gospel of thy peace are girt,
The belt from which doth hang the Spirit's sword,
Shall breathe on dead bones, and the bones shall live,
Sweet poison to the evil self shall give,
And, clean themselves, lift men clean from the mire abhorred.

ELEVEN

My Lord, I have no clothes to come to thee;
My shoes are pierced and broken with the road;
I am torn and weathered, wounded with the goad,
And soiled with tugging at my weary load:

The more I need thee! A very prodigal
I stagger into thy presence, Lord of me:
One look, my Christ, and at thy feet I fall!

TWELVE

Why should I still hang back, like one in a dream,
Who vainly strives to clothe himself aright,
That in great presence he may seemly seem?
Why call up feeling-dress me in the faint,
Worn, faded, cast-off nimbus of some saint?
Why of old mood bring back a ghostly gleam—
While there he waits, love's heart and loss's blight!

THIRTEEN

Son of the Father, elder brother mine,
See thy poor brother's plight! See how he stands
Defiled and feeble, hanging down his hands!
Make me clean, brother, with thy burning shine;
From thy rich treasures, householder divine,
Bring forth fair garments, old and new, I pray,
And like thy brother dress me, in the old home-bred way.

FOURTEEN

My prayer-bird was cold—would not away,
Although I set it on the edge of the nest.
Then I bethought me of the story old—
Love-fact or loving fable, thou know'st best—
How, when the children had made sparrows of clay,
Thou mad'st them birds, with wings to flutter and fold:
Take, Lord, my prayer in thy hand, and make it pray.

FIFTEEN

My poor clay-sparrow seems turned to a stone,
And from my heart will neither fly nor run.
I cannot feel as thou and I both would,
But, Father, I am willing—make me good.

What art thou Father for, but to help thy son?
Look deep, yet deeper, in my heart, and there,
Beyond where I can feel, read thou the prayer.

SIXTEEN

Oh, what it were to be right sure of thee!
Sure that thou art, and the same as thy son, Jesus!
Oh, faith is deeper, wider than the sea,
Yea, than the blue of heaven that ever flees us!
Yet simple as the cry of sore-hurt child,
Or as his shout, with sudden gladness wild,
When home from school he runs, till morn set free.

SEVENTEEN

If I were sure thou, Father, verily art,
True father of the Nazarene as true,
Sure as I am of my wife's shielding heart,
Sure as of sunrise in the watching blue,
Sure as I am that I do eat and drink,
And have a heart to love and laugh and think,
Meseems in flame the joy might from my body start.

EIGHTEEN

But I must know thee in a deeper way
Than any of these ways, or know thee not;
My heart at peace far loftier proof must lay
Than if the wind thou me the wave didst roll,
Than if I lay before thee a sunny spot,
Or knew thee as the body knows its soul,
Or even as the part doth know its perfect whole.

NINETEEN

There is no word to tell how I must know thee;
No wind clasped ever a low meadow-flower
So close that as to nearness it could show thee;
No rainbow so makes one the sun and shower.

A something with thee, I am a nothing fro' thee
Because I am not save as I am in thee,
My soul is ever setting out to win thee.

TWENTY

I know not how—for that I first must know thee.
I know I know thee not as I would know thee,
For my heart burns like theirs that did not know him,
Till he broke bread, and therein they must know him.
I know thee, knowing that I do not know thee,
Nor ever shall till one with me I know thee—
Even as thy Son, the eternal man, doth know thee.

TWENTY-ONE

Creation under me, in, and above,
Slopes upward from the base, a pyramid,
On whose point I shall stand at last, and love
From the first rush of vapor at thy will,
To the last poet-word that darkness chid,
Thou hast been sending up creation's hill,
To lift thy souls aloft in faithful Godhead free.

TWENTY-TWO

I think my thought, and fancy I think thee.
Lord, wake me up; rend swift my coffin-planks;
I pray thee, let me live—alive and free.
My soul will break forth in melodious thanks,
Aware at last what thou wouldst have it be,
When thy life shall be light in me, and when
My life to thine is answer and amen.

TWENTY-THREE

How oft I say the same things in these lines!
Even as a man, buried in during dark,
Turns ever where the edge of twilight shines,
Prays ever towards the vague eternal mark;

Or as the sleeper, having dreamed he drinks,
Back straightway into thirstful dreaming sinks,
So turns my will to thee, for thee still longs, still pines.

TWENTY-FOUR

The mortal man, all careful, wise, and troubled,
The eternal child in the nursery doth keep.
Tomorrow on today the man heaps doubled;
The child laughs, hopeful, even in his sleep.
The man rebukes the child for foolish trust;
The child replies, "Thy care is for poor dust;
Be still, and let me wake that thou mayst sleep."

TWENTY-FIVE

Till I am one, with oneness manifold,
I must breed contradiction, strife, and doubt;
Things tread thy court—look real—take proving hold—
My Christ is not yet grown to cast them out;
Alas, to me, false-judging 'twixt the twain,
The *Unseen* oft fancy seems, while, all about,
The *Seen* doth lord it with a mighty train.

TWENTY-SIX

But when the Will hath learned obedience royal,
He straight will set the child upon the throne;
To whom the seen things all, grown instant loyal,
Will gather to his feet, in homage prone—
The child their master they have ever known;
Then shall the visible fabric plainly lean
On a Reality that never can be seen.

TWENTY-SEVEN

Thy ways are wonderful, Maker of men!
Thou gavest me a child, and I have fed
And clothed and loved her, many a growing year;
Lo, now a friend of months draws gently near,

And claims her future—all beyond his ken—
There he hath never loved her nor hath led:
She weeps and moans, but turns, and leaves her home so dear.

TWENTY-EIGHT

She leaves, but not forsakes. Oft in the night,
Oft at mid-day when all is still around,
Sudden will rise, in dim pathetic light,
Some childish memory of household bliss,
Or sorrow by love's service robed and crowned;
Rich in his love, she yet will sometimes miss
The mother's folding arms, the mother's sealing kiss.

TWENTY-NINE

Then first, I think, our eldest-born, although
Loving, devoted, tender, watchful, dear,
The innermost of home-bred love shall know!
Yea, when at last the janitor draws near,
A still, pale joy will through the darkness go,
At thought of lying in those arms again,
Which once were heaven enough for any pain.

THIRTY

By love doth love grow mighty in its love:
Once thou shalt love us, child, as we love thee.
Father of loves, is it not thy decree
That, by our long, far-wandering remove
From thee, our life, our home, our being blest,
We learn at last to love thee true and best,
And rush with all our loves back to thy infinite rest!

DECEMBER

Of two to make one, which yet two shall be,
Is thy creation's problem, deep, and true,
To which thou only hold'st the happy, hurting clue.

December

One

I AM A LITTLE WEARY OF MY LIFE—
Not thy life, blessed Father! Or the blood
Too slowly laves the coral shores of thought,
Or I am weary of weariness and strife.
Open my soul-gates to thy living flood;
I ask not larger heart-throbs, vigor-fraught,
I pray thy presence, with strong patience rife.

Two

I will what thou will'st—only keep me sure
That thou art willing; call to me now and then.
So, ceasing to enjoy, I shall endure
With perfect patience—willing beyond my ken,
Beyond my love, beyond my thinking scope;
Willing to be because thy will is pure;
Willing thy will beyond all bounds of hope.

Three

This weariness of mine, may it not come
From something that doth need no setting right?
Shall fruit be blamed if it hang wearily
A day before it perfected drop plumb

To the sad earth from off its nursing tree?
Ripeness must always come with loss of might,
The weary evening fall before the resting night.

FOUR

Hither if I have come through earth and air,
Through fire and water—I am not of them;
Born in the darkness, what fair-flashing gem
Would to the earth go back and nestle there?
Not of this world, this world my life doth hem;
What if I weary, then, and look to the door,
Because my unknown life is swelling at the core?

FIVE

All winged things came from the waters first;
Airward still many a one from the water springs
In dens and caves wind-loving things are nursed:
I lie like unhatched bird, upfolded, dumb,
While all the air is trembling with the hum
Of songs and beating hearts and whirring wings,
That call my slumbering life to wake to happy things.

SIX

I lay last night and knew not why I was sad.
"'Tis well with God," I said, "and he is the truth;
Let that content me." 'Tis not strength, nor youth,
Nor buoyant health, nor a heart merry-mad,
That makes the fact of things wherein men live:
He is the life, and doth my life outgive;
In him there is no gloom, but all is solemn-glad.

SEVEN

I said to myself, "Lo, I lie in a dream
Of separation, where there comes no sign;
My waking life is hid with Christ in God,
Where all is true and potent—fact divine."

I will not heed the thing that doth but seem;
I will be quiet as lark upon the sod;
God's will, the seed, shall rest in me the pod.

EIGHT

And when that will shall blossom—then, my God,
There will be jubilation in a world!
The glad lark, soaring heaven-ward from the sod,
Up the swift spiral of its own song whirled,
Never such jubilation wild out-poured
As from my soul will break at thy feet, Lord,
Like a great tide from sea-heart shoreward hurled.

NINE

For then thou wilt be able, then at last,
To glad me as thou hungerest to do;
Then shall thy life my heart all open find,
A thoroughfare to thy great spirit-wind;
Then shall I rest within thy holy vast,
One with the bliss of the eternal mind;
And all creation rise in me created new.

TEN

What makes thy being a bliss shall then make mine
For I shall love as thou, and love in thee;
Then shall I have whatever I desire,
My every faintest wish being all divine;
Power thou wilt give me to work mightily,
Even as my Lord, leading thy low men nigher,
With dance and song to cast their best upon thy fire.

ELEVEN

Then shall I live such an essential life
That a mere flower will then to me unfold
More bliss than now grandest orchestral strife—
By love made and obedience humble-bold,

I shall straight through its window God behold.
God, I shall feed on thee, thy creature blest
With very being—work at one with sweetest rest.

TWELVE

Give me a world, to part for praise and sunder.
The brooks be bells; the winds, in caverns dumb,
Wake fife and flute and flageolet and voice;
The fire-shook earth itself be the great drum;
And let the air the region's bass out thunder;
The firs be violins; the reeds hautboys;
Rivers, seas, icebergs fill the great score up and under!

THIRTEEN

But rather dost thou hear the blundered words
Of breathing creatures; the music-lowing herds
Of thy great cattle; thy soft-bleating sheep;
O'erhovered by the trebles of thy birds,
Whose Christ-praised carelessness song-fills the deep;
Still rather a child's talk who apart doth hide him,
And make a tent for God to come and sit beside him.

FOURTEEN

This is not life; this being is not enough.
But thou art life, and thou hast life for me.
Thou mad'st the worm—to cast the wormy slough,
And fly abroad—a glory flit and flee.
Thou hast me, statue-like, hewn in the rough,
Meaning at last to shape me perfectly.
Lord, thou hast called me forth, I turn and call on thee.

FIFTEEN

'Tis thine to make, mine to rejoice in thine,
As, hungering for his mother's face and eyes,
The child throws wide the door, back to the wall,
I run to thee, the refuge from poor lies:

Lean dogs behind me whimper, yelp, and whine;
Life lieth ever sick, Death's writhing thrall,
In slavery endless, hopeless, and supine.

SIXTEEN

The life that hath not willed itself to be,
Must clasp the life that willed, and be at peace;
Or, like a leaf wind-blown, through chaos flee;
A life-husk into which the demons go,
And work their will, and drive it to and fro;
A thing that neither is, nor yet can cease,
Which uncreation can alone release.

SEVENTEEN

But when I turn and grasp the making hand,
And will the making will, with confidence
I ride the crest of the creation-wave,
Helpless no more, no more existence' slave;
In the heart of love's creating fire I stand,
And, love-possessed in heart and soul and sense,
Take up the making share the making Master gave.

EIGHTEEN

That man alone who does the Father's works
Can be the Father's son; yea, only he
Who sonlike can create, can ever *be;*
Who with God wills not, is no son, not free.
O Father, send the demon-doubt that lurks
Behind the hope, out into the abyss;
Who trusts in knowledge all its good shall miss.

NINETEEN

Thy beasts are sinless, and do live before thee;
Thy child is sinful, and must run to thee.
Thy angels sin not, and in peace adore thee;
But I must will, or never more be free.

I from thy heart came, how can I ignore thee?
Back to my home I hurry, haste, and flee;
There I shall dwell, love-praising evermore thee.

TWENTY

My holy self, thy pure ideal, lies
Calm in thy bosom, which it cannot leave;
My self unholy, no ideal, hies
Hither and thither, gathering store to grieve—
Not *now*, O Father! Now it mounts, it flies,
To join the true self in thy heart that waits,
And, one with it, be one with all the heavenly mates.

TWENTY-ONE

Trusting thee, Christ, I kneel, and clasp thy knee;
Cast myself down, and kiss thy brother-feet—
One self thou and the Father's thought of thee!
Ideal son, thou hast left the perfect home,
Ideal brother, to seek thy brothers come!
Thou know'st our angels all, God's children sweet,
And of each two wilt make one holy child complete.

TWENTY-TWO

To a slow end I draw these daily words,
Nor think such words often to write again—
Rather, as light the power to me affords,
Christ's new and old would to my friends unbind;
Through words be spoke help to his thought behind;
Unveil the heart with which he drew his men;
Set forth his rule o'er devils, animals, corn, and wind.

TWENTY-THREE

I do remember how one time I thought,
"God must be lonely—oh, so lonely lone!
I will be very good to him—ah, nought
Can reach the heart of his great loneliness!

My whole heart I will bring him, with a moan
That I may not come nearer; I will lie prone
Before the awful loveliness in loneliness' excess."

TWENTY-FOUR

A God must have a God for company.
And lo, thou hast the Son-God to thy friend.
Thou honor'st his obedience, he thy law.
Into thy secret life-will he doth see;
Thou fold'st him round in live love perfectly—
One two, without beginning, without end;
In love, life, strength, and truth, perfect without a flaw.

TWENTY-FIVE

Thou hast not made, or taught me, Lord, to care
For times and seasons—but this one glad day
Is the blue sapphire clasping all the lights
That flash in the girdle of the year so fair—
When thou wast born a man, because alway
Thou wast and art a man, through all the flights
Of thought, and time, and thousandfold creation's play.

TWENTY-SIX

We all are lonely, Maker—each a soul
Shut in by itself, a sundered atom of thee.
No two yet loved themselves into a whole;
Even when we weep together we are two.
Of two to make one, which yet two shall be,
Is thy creation's problem, deep, and true,
To which thou only hold'st the happy, hurting clue.

TWENTY-SEVEN

No less than thou, O Father, do we need
A God to friend each lonely one of us.
As touch not in the sack two grains of seed,
Touch no two hearts in great worlds populous.

Outside the making God we cannot meet
Him he has made our brother: homeward, thus,
To find our kin we first must turn our wandering feet.

TWENTY-EIGHT

It must be possible that the soul made
Should absolutely meet the soul that makes;
Then, in that bearing soul, meet every other
There also born, each sister and each brother.
Lord, till I meet thee thus, life is delayed;
I am not I until that morning breaks,
Not I until my consciousness eternal wakes.

TWENTY-NINE

Again I shall behold thee, daughter true;
The hour will come when I shall hold thee fast
In God's name, loving thee all through and through.
Somewhere in his grand thought this waits for us.
Then shall I see a smile not like thy last—
For that great thing which came when all was past,
Was not a smile, but God's peace glorious.

THIRTY

Twilight of the transfiguration-joy,
Gleam-faced, pure-eyed, strong-willed, high-hearted boy!
Hardly thy life clear forth of heaven was sent,
Ere it broke out into a smile, and went.
So swift thy growth, so true thy goalward bent,
Thou, child and sage inextricably blent,
Wilt one day teach thy father in some heavenly tent.

THIRTY-ONE

Go, my beloved children, live your life.
Wounded, faint, bleeding, never yield the strife.
Stunned, fallen-awake, arise, and fight again.
Before you victory stands, with shining train

Of hopes not credible until they *are.*
Beyond morass and mountain swells the star
Of perfect love—the home of longing heart and brain.

ENDNOTES

INTRODUCTION

[1] Rolland Hein, Ed., Introduction, *The Heart of George MacDonald* (Wheaton: Harold Shaw Publishers, 1994), xvii.

[2] Rolland Hein, *George MacDonald: Victorian Mythmaker* (Nashville: StarSong Publishing Group, 1993), 319.

SUGGESTED READING

DOCHERTY, JOHN. *The Literary Products of the Lewis Carroll—George MacDonald Friendship.* New York: Edwin Mellen Press, 1995.

ELLISON, ROBERT. *The Victorian Pulpit.* Cranbury, NJ: Associated University Presses, 1998.

FINK, LARRY. *George MacDonald: Images of His World.* Abilene, Texas: Pasture Spring Press, 2004.

HEIN, ROLLAND. *George MacDonald: Victorian Mythmaker.* Nashville: StarSong Publishing Group, 1993.

———. *The Heart of George MacDonald: An Anthology.* Colorado Springs: Harold Shaw Publishers, 1994.

LARSON, TIMOTHY. *Contested Christianity: The Political and Social Contexts of Victorian Theology.* Waco: Baylor University Press, 2004.

LEWIS, C. S., ED. *George MacDonald: 365 Readings.* New York: Collier Books, 1947.

MACDONALD, GEORGE. *The Complete Fairy Tales.* New York: Penguin Classics, 1999.

———. *The Curate of Glaston: Three Dramatic Novels.* Minneapolis: Bethany House, 2002.

———. *George MacDonald in the Pulpit: Compilation of Spoken Sermons, 1871–1901.* United Kingdom: Johannesen, 1997.

———. *Phantastes.* Grand Rapids: William B. Eerdmans, 1981.

———. *The Unspoken Sermons—Series I, II, and III.* United Kingdom: Johannesen, 1997.

MACDONALD, GREVILLE. *George MacDonald and His Wife.* London: George Allen & Unwin, Ltd., 1924.

PRICKETT, STEPHEN. *Victorian Fantasy* revised ed. Waco: Baylor, 2005.

Look for the following titles, available now from
The Barnes & Noble Library of Essential Reading.

Visit your Barnes & Noble bookstore,
or shop online at *www.bn.com/loer*

NONFICTION

Tragic Sense of Life	Miguel de Unamuno	0760777764
Travels of Marco Polo, The	Marco Polo	0760765898
Treatise Concerning the Principles of Human Knowledge, A	George Berkeley	0760777691
Treatise of Human Nature, A	David Hume	0760771723
Trial and Death of Socrates, The	Plato	0760762007
Up From Slavery	Booker T. Washington	0760752346
Utilitarianism	William James	0760771758
Vindication of the Rights of Woman, A	Mary Wollstonecraft	0760754942
Violin Playing As I Teach It	Leopold Auer	0760749914
Voyage of the *Beagle*, The	Charles Darwin	0760754969
Wealth of Nations, The	Adam Smith	0760757615
Wilderness Hunter, The	Theodore Roosevelt	0760756031
Will to Believe and Human Immortality, The	William James	0760770190
Will to Power, The	Friedrich Nietzsche	0760777772
Worst Journey in the World, The	Aspley Cherry-Garrard	0760757593
You Know Me Al	Ring W. Lardner	0760758336

THE BARNES & NOBLE
LIBRARY OF ESSENTIAL READING

This newly developed series has been established to provide affordable access to books of literary, academic, and historic value—works of both well-known writers and those who deserve to be rediscovered. Selected and introduced by scholars and specialists with an intimate knowledge of the works, these volumes present complete, original texts in a modern, readable typeface— welcoming a new generation of readers to influential and important books of the past. With more than 100 titles already in print and more than 100 forthcoming, the Library of Essential Reading offers an unrivaled variety of thought, scholarship, and entertainment. Best of all, these handsome and durable paperbacks are priced to be exceptionally affordable. For a full list of titles, visit *www.bn.com/loer*.